BARBECUE BOOK

Editor: R. Arthur Barrett
by
E. W. (Wade) BUSBY
R. A. (Art) Barrett

BOOK TRADE DISTRIBUTION BY
GROSSET & DUNLAP, INC.
NEW YORK CITY, N.Y. 10010

TESTED RECIPE INSTITUTE, INC. CHICAGO, ILLINOIS 60648

contents

REVISED EDITION

ISBN 0-88352-000-1

Library of Congress Catalog Card Number 63-12737

Kitchen in the Clouds®

Litho in U.S.A.

how it all began

Back in the days of cave men and wandering tribes—when cooking first began—men used to roast or broil their food in the open air. There was no other way to do it. Pioneers, cowboys, and hunters also barbecued, not as a hobby or diversion, but just to eat.

As time went on, for most of us, cooking over an open fire was no longer a necessity. Modern inventions brought gas and electric ranges into the kitchen. Still, there's something of the rugged outdoorsman in every American—there's a feeling of adventure and good fellowship about a barbecue that helps to explain its tremendous popularity.

In Texas and other parts of the West and South, there grew up the custom of huge parties, sometimes for thousands of people, where first buffalo and later hogs and cattle were roasted whole, served with mountains of bread and barrels of beer. These "ox-roasts" were usually accompanied with fireworks, games, races, and square dancing—a good time for all.

Today, millions who know that there is no substitute for the true tangy flavor of a barbecued steak are holding equally festive outdoor parties on a much smaller scale.

And it's no wonder barbecues are becoming so popular! They are recognized as the graceful, informal way to entertain. Whether on a penthouse garden, a cool patio, a shady lawn or at the beach, it's a chance in the summer for a woman to get out of the hot kitchen into the open air where cooking is a pleasure and the men often take over.

More and more, people are realizing that the fun of a barbecue needn't be restricted to the summer months—that late fall and early spring cook-outs are exciting because of the feel of the crisp air and the smell of the char-barbecued meats. Even in the winter, a barbecue in the garage, a breezeway or any other sheltered spot is possible and fun too.

We at Tested Recipe Institute, Inc. have selected Big Boy Equipment because we know it is exceptionally fine and will give excellent barbecuing results with a minimum of work and expense. Purchase good quality meats, poultry and other food in order to make the barbecue an occasion which will be long remembered.

how to select equipment

The barbecue equipment that will give you the most pleasure and excitement should be quality-built and with the essential features that will bring you and your family real enjoyment.

important features

High quality heavy duty steel for durably constructed fire box, hood, legs and braces.

Grill made of steel plated with nickel and chrome for beauty and long life. Closely spaced rods to hold even the smallest foods.

Heavy duty spit assembly with a heavy duty motor with triple prong plug to assure you safety in operation. Spit should rotate 6 RPM clockwise for proper self-basting. Spit rod should be 5/16" square. Spit forks should be made of heavy spring steel. Rod and forks should have nickel and chrome plated finish.

Mechanism for raising and lowering grill or fire box should have positive screw action and be sturdy and well constructed, see page 9. A make-shift mechanism may result in spoiling expensive meats.

Quality hood of heavy duty bonderized steel for strength and to hold and reflect heat. Hood is designed for maximum size food using a minimum of fuel. Unique barrel-type design (Fig. 1 & 2) circulates live heat through-out covered area for fast, even cooking, sealing in natural meat juices.

Brazier hood should be of heavy duty bonderized steel for strength and beauty. Hood should extend forward of lift rod (Fig. 3). The spit should be recessed back into the hood. This deeper hood insures a much better job of barbecuing. It permits you on a charcoal grill (Fig. 3) to place drip pan under meat in front of bowl to catch juices for gravy or sauces. On a gas fired brazier the foods turn over the porcelainized dome. Juices drip on the dome and burn to give foods that "open air" barbecue flavor. These deep hoods protect the meat from the wind which dissipates heat and prevents foods from barbecuing evenly.

Equipment having these features will add to your pride of ownership and give you years of barbecuing pleasure. Your barbecue center is a family investment, therefore, buy those features which will best serve your family's needs. Price alone is false economy. Make Barbecuing a Family Pastime.

Fig. 1

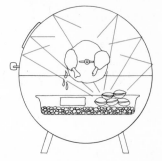

Fig. 2

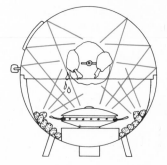

Fig. 3

the fun of barbecuing

Pull up the benches and have a big crowd. You can entertain 15 or 20 outdoors with less trouble than it takes for six in the dining room, and with less strain on the budget. On weekends outdoor breakfasts are fun too.

Husbands become the experts and do the barbecuing. Wives take it easy. All they have to do is make the salad and dessert. The kitchen stays clean. The house remains neat. There is almost no wash-up afterwards.

So economical, too! Serve your friends fine barbecues. The cost is only about $1.50 a person instead of about $6.95 for the same meal in a restaurant.

Be the Barbecue Leader in your neighborhood. Your friends will call you the best host in town. Then they'll invite you to their backyards after they've learned your tricks of entertaining in the great outdoors.

Take your grill to the beach, park on outings and camping trips, its the thing to do.

Everybody pitches in and enjoys the "get-ready" as well as the eating. New acquaintances and neighbors are like old friends after you've cooked a meal together.

You can laugh at bumper-to-bumper traffic on steaming highways as you play host in your own backyard. All the comforts of home, plus the carefree, informal fun of the picnics you loved in childhood!

how to plan a barbecue

There is only one way in which a barbecue bears any resemblance to other forms of entertaining, and that is the need for planning ahead.

A few quiet moments with pencil and paper will do away with headaches and confusion on the day of the barbecue. Supplies won't run short, food won't be wasted, serving and clean-up will be simplified enormously, and everyone will have a good time.

First comes the menu. Keep it simple and easy to manage. Put most of the emphasis on the barbecued food and limit other courses to chilled juice cocktail, a crisp salad, an easy-to-eat dessert that can be made ahead of time (such as cake, pie, cookies or ice cream cones) and plenty of coffee or tea, hot or iced depending on the season. You will find many such menu suggestions scattered throughout this book.

Next comes the market order. Gauge amounts by the length of your guest list. Plan on two helpings of barbecued foods, but buy enough so that, if a couple of trenchermen are present, they can have three! The information in the section on "How Much Meat to Buy" will help you decide.

Now make a list of all the preparation jobs that can be done ahead of time—dessert, salad ingredients, breads, etc. Then list on-the-spot jobs and jot down a name opposite each so everyone can get in the act.

Check all of your barbecuing and serving equipment to be sure that everything is in good condition.

Whenever possible (and it usually is) use paper dishes and cups to make clean-up easy. Choose sturdy, plastic-coated plates that won't disintegrate when hot food is served on them, and get special strong paper cups for hot beverages—never use wax coated cups except for cold beverages. Man-sized, tough paper napkins, and plenty of them, are a must for barbecues. Use stainless steel table cutlery with raffa-wrapped or bright plastic handles to spare your fine silver.

If it rains, set up the equipment in a breezeway or a well-ventilated garage. Fun for everyone in all kinds of weather . . . bright breezy spring days, lazy summer evenings when daylight lingers long, crisp blue and gold autumn weather, sunlit frosty winter days . . . even when it rains or snows . . . because a barbecue awakens the gypsy in all of us with its light-hearted informality and comradeship.

check list

for the fire

For Charcoal Grill
Gravel
Charcoal briquets
Charcoal lighter fluid
Electric fire starter
Fire rake
Fire tongs
Pail of water (for quenching briquets)
Asbestos gloves
Small shovel
Smoke chips
Matches

For Gas Fired Brazier
Matches
Asbestos gloves
Smoke chips

for spit barbecuing

Spit motor
Spit rod
Spit forks
Spit basket
Skewers
Heavy twine
Hammer
Pliers
Heavy duty aluminum foil
Meat thermometer
Heavy duty extension cord
Basting brush

for grill barbecuing

Tongs
Skewers
Heavy duty foil
Basting brush

for handling food

Long-handled fork
Long-handled spatula
Long-handled steak tongs

things you may need

Salt and pepper and other seasonings you
   may want
Pans (for sauces, etc.)
Coffee pot
Carving board or small butcher's block
Carving knife and fork
Platters
Salad bowl
Salad servers or tongs
Trays
Paper plates and cups
Paper napkins
Paper toweling
Paper disposal bags
Knives, forks and spoons
Ice bucket
Thermos
Folding chairs and table
Apron
Sponge
Cover to protect grill when not in use

my own list

Guest list

_____
_____
_____
_____
_____
_____
_____
_____
_____
_____
_____

how to build a fire

Charcoal broiling is man's favorite way to prepare steaks and other meat. Good charcoal fires are easy to make and use if you carefully study and follow the information below and on the following pages.

facts about charcoal briquets

High quality charcoal briquets produced by reputable nationally advertised manufacturers are made from maple, birch, beech and oak trees. These briquets are superior because they are made from hardwoods which are dense and have a low resin content. This results in charcoal briquets which have a minimum of tar and therefore smoke less and have little odor.

We believe the charcoal flavor comes from the acrid light blue smoke which is given off in the initial burning stage of charcoal. Add a few pieces of charcoal or briquets to the fire during the cooking period to enhance this flavor. Be sure you have burned all lighter fuel or impregnated starter odors out of your fire before you start to cook as the kerosene or petroleum odors will spoil the flavor of the food.

Six tons of green, fresh-cut wood is required to produce about one ton of charcoal. The hardwood logs are cut up into chips and placed in a dryer where the heat removes the moisture from the wood. The dry chips are then carbonized into charcoal in huge retorts with a heat of 700 to 900 degrees. Direct flames do not come in contact with the wood chips. The charcoal is then cooled, pulverized, mixed with a binder, and compressed to form the briquets. These briquets are very hard and dense. They will burn for a long period of time giving intense,

even heat without "pop sparks." High quality charcoal briquets are essential for a successful barbecue and in the long run will prove to be economical.

facts about other charcoals

Ordinary soft wood or wood scrap charcoal can be used. This charcoal is made by charring wood in a kiln. It comes in varying size chunks, and has a tendency to sputter and smoke and may give the food an undesirable flavor because of a high resin content. Often it will give off "pop sparks" and heat from it may be uneven. If you have difficulty in starting the fire, next time try a different brand of fuel.

we recommend

Hardwood charcoal briquets give the best results and the most uniform barbecuing. Charcoal and charcoal briquets must be stored in a dry place so they will not absorb moisture and become difficult to light.

properly designed equipment

fire box of big boy barrels

All Big Boy Barrel Units have specially designed fire boxes of heavy duty cold rolled steel (see Fig. 1). These units have a positive worm gear-ratchet to raise and lower the fire box (see Fig. 2). Fire box is held firmly at both ends for accurate, safe adjustment. This gear-ratchet is the device for regulating heat. The circular design of the barrel travels the heat over, under and around the food for perfect results everytime.

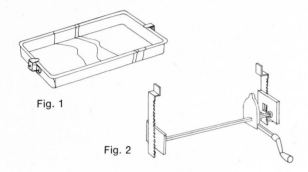

Fig. 1

Fig. 2

fire bowl of big boy braziers

The Big Boy new revolutionary Jumbo "Roll Rim Bowls" have a massive look and are bigger, deeper and strong (see Fig. 3). They are made of heavy duty one-piece die formed steel with a bonderized baked-on finish. They have an extra rib for greater rigidity and a flat bottom for convenience. Raising and lowering the grill is by means of a positive screw-type mechanism (see Fig. 4). This gives you control of heat intensity during grilling. When using the brazier for spit barbecuing, the heat intensity is controlled by raising or lowering the motor-spit assembly in the 3-position spit notches on the hood (see Fig. 5).

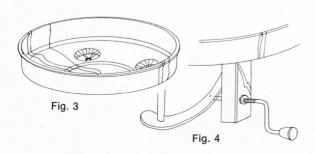

Fig. 3

Fig. 4

Fig. 5

fire bowl of big boy gas fired braziers

The "Roll Rim Bowls" have been designed for the gas units. A large opening and rock retaining ring have been added to accommodate the new circular cast-iron burner and Bar-B-Rocks. A porcelainized Guardian Dome has been added to keep the gas ports clear and to direct the flame onto the Bar-B-Rocks (see Fig. 6).

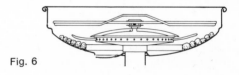

Fig. 6

use of gravel or fire base

A gravel base permits the charcoal fire to "breathe" and gives a more even heat distribution. In the brazier bowl use enough gravel to make the bed level out to the rib at the edge of the bowl. In the barrel type units cover the fire box with gravel from ¾ to 1 inch deep (see Fig. 7).

Before putting gravel in the charcoal bowl or fire box, line it with aluminum foil. This gives added fuel economy, reflects the heat and makes cleaning easier. After four to six barbecues, wash the gravel in hot sudsy water; spread it out to dry. Some gravel "pops" if used when wet, so be sure you dry it before using it again. If you wish you can use commercial insulating fire base. We prefer pea gravel as it is easier to handle the fire, the coals don't sink into the base.

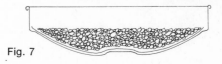

Fig. 7

how to build a fire

liquid fire starters

Follow the manufacturers directions. Arrange a pyramid of about 15 briquets on the fire base of your fire bowl or fire box. Squirt about ½ cup of the fire starter on the cold briquets. Reseal the container and place it away from the grill. Light the briquets with a match (long match if available). Your fire is ready when briquets are covered with gray ash (30 to 45 minutes). Never add lighter fluid to a fire which is burning or to briquets which are warm, this could be dangerous.

how charcoal burns

Because charcoal briquets ignite first in small areas you may think the briquets are not burning. But look closely and you will see tiny gray spots which show where the briquets are burning. To prove to yourself that these gray areas are actually burning, pick up a briquet with a pair of tongs, blow on it and you will see a red glow.

As the briquets burn, a deposit of fine ash is left on the surface of the coals. The heat is released through the ash in the form of infrared rays. In the daytime, the red glow is not normally visible, but when barbecuing with a hood it is sometimes possible to see the glow. At night the red glow is visible.

portable electric fire starters

Arrange briquets over an area about 8 by 12 inches. Place heating element of the Fire Starter on the fuel, then put a pyramid of briquets on the element a few inches high. Plug fire starter into appliance outlet. After a few minutes gray ash will appear on briquets around the heating element. After 7 to 10 minutes disconnect and remove fire starter. Wait about 15 minutes until briquets are well covered with gray ash. Arrange fire as indicated on page 11.

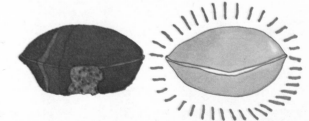

gray ash insulates

Remove this gray ash just before starting to barbecue. Tap the coals lightly with a fire rake or poker. It is also advisable to tap the briquets occasionally during barbecuing to remove the ash. Experiment by putting your hand over briquets that are ash covered. Then tap off the ash and again put your hand over them. Feel how much more heat you have. By this simple device, you often avoid adding more fuel near the end of the barbecuing.

when to start your fire

A good barbecue chef starts his fire far enough in advance to get a good bed of coals before beginning to barbecue. When using an Electric Fire Starter, allow about 15 minutes. With other fire starters, allow about 45 minutes. This permits time for the briquets to develop intense heat to cook food properly.

how to add charcoal briquets

Put a supply of briquets in the fire bowl or box, at the edge, to warm up. Add warm briquets about 15 minutes before you need them. Do not dump cold briquets on live ones. This reduces the temperature of the fire and retards barbecuing.

to avoid flame-up

When grill cooking space briquets ½ inch apart to reduce flame-up. When spit cooking keep fire well to the rear (see Fig. 3, Fig. 4 this page).

how to arrange briquets

Start barbecuing when the charcoal briquets are covered with a fine gray ash. This takes about 15 minutes with the Electric Fire Starter and about 45 minutes with other starters. There will be no visible flame.

arrange briquets for the spit

Heap briquets in a pile toward the rear of the brazier bowl (see Fig. 1) or fire box (see Fig. 2). Tap briquets to remove the gray ash. Then, set a drip pan in front of them (see page 14). Attach spit and start the motor.

On the barrel close the hood. Control the amount of heat during barbecuing by adjusting the height of the fire box in barrels or the height of the motor-driven spit on braziers. After barbecuing starts, adjust position of drip pan to catch juices which drip from the lowest part of the meat.

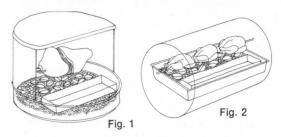

Fig. 1   Fig. 2

arrange briquets for the grill

Spread briquets over gravel in brazier (see Fig. 3) or in fire box (see Fig. 4), leaving about ½″ space between briquets to avoid flame-up. This arrangement will give you the proper heat for grilling. If fire is not used at once, tap briquets to remove gray ash just before starting to barbecue.

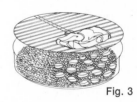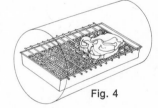

Fig. 3   Fig. 4

how to estimate temperature

To estimate temperature at grill level, hold hand cautiously, palm side down, just above grill and judge temperature by number of seconds hand can be kept in position. Count seconds this way:

1000—1
1000—2—**HIGH** or Hot
1000—3—**MEDIUM-HIGH** or Medium Hot
1000—4—**MEDIUM**
1000—5—**MEDIUM-LOW**
1000—6—**LOW**

These temperatures are used in the recipes in this book and are shown in **BOLD** type. These same temperatures approximate the dial markings on most gas grills.

To estimate temperature at spit level, hold hand cautiously palm side down, just below roast on spit and proceed as for grill level above.

gas fired braziers

Barbecuing on a Gas Fired Grill is not a great deal different than cooking on a Charcoal Grill. It takes all the romance and flavor of old-time "open air" barbecuing and adds the convenience and dependability of gas fuel.

If you are using the SPIT OR SHISH-KABAB skewers remove the grill. Light the fire and you are ready to barbecue.

If you are using the GRILL light the fire and preheat the Bar-B-Rocks on the **HIGH** setting for about 3 minutes. Turn control to **MEDIUM** or **LOW.** Remember the longer you cook on a lower heat after preheating the more you will have to adjust the flame to maintain heat.

Remember the real Western Barbecue is slow "Open Air" cooking. Never rush it by using **HIGH** heat. The **HIGH** heat position is only for preheating the Bar-B-Rocks or for short periods to bring the heat up to barbecuing temperature.

As you gain experience with the constant heat you get with gas you will learn to increase the heat slightly until you have the heat you like best.

Excessive flame-up is a sign of too high a heat. Reduce flame by turning Burner Control to a lower setting or rotate revolving grill to remove food from area of flame-up.

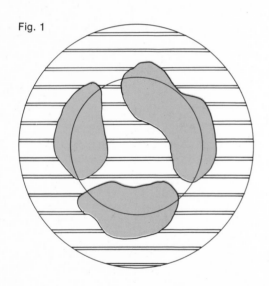

Fig. 1

Place food to be grill barbecued on the grill directly over the circle of flame above dome (Fig. 1). If you are cooking for a crowd use the whole grill and leave about 1 inch of space around outer edge of grill. This will give you an umbrella of even heat (Fig. 2) over the entire grill area.

heat guide

Heat settings in this book are in **BOLD** type.

HEAT SETTING	USE FOR
LOW	Keeping foods warm. Heating breads.
MEDIUM-LOW	Holding spit-cooked foods at serving temperature. Use this setting when fire gets too hot. Safe for slow grilling and spit barbecuing.
MEDIUM	Good all around setting. For spit barbecuing roast or poultry. Grilling thin chops or hamburgers.
MEDIUM-HIGH	For spit cooking or grilling on cool days. If heat is too low use this setting to bring heat up to barbecuing temperature.
HIGH	Only use this heat for brief periods 2 to 5 minutes. For preheating unit. For searing steaks and chops.

Fig. 2

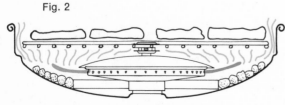

what affects barbecuing time

kind of fuel

Charcoal briquets burn with an intense, even heat for a long period of time. Inferior fuels may burn too fast or too slowly. Poor fuels may sputter and smoke, "pop spark" or flame and you will miss the true charcoal flavor. You can easily spoil an expensive cut of meat by experimenting with unproven fuels. With good charcoal briquets giving the same even heat each time, you will learn to depend on them for more exact timing of your barbecued foods.

amount of fuel

The degree of heat from charcoal briquets depends on how many briquets are used and how closely they are placed together. Learn how to use a modest quantity.

size and shape of meat

Barbecuing time will vary considerably depending on the size and shape of the meat to be barbecued.

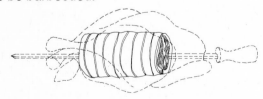

distance of food from heat

Place your hand close to burning charcoal briquets and gradually draw it away. You will see that the distance of the food from the heat will make a lot of difference.

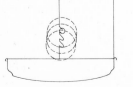

wind velocity and direction

The hood of your Big Boy unit will protect the food from the wind. To prevent the top of the meat from cooling while the underside is barbecuing, turn the back of the hood into the wind.

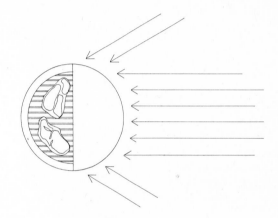

because of these factors

All barbecuing times given are estimates based on average conditions. Keep records of what you do for your own future guidance.

when in a hurry

Build a fire following one of the methods described on page 10. When the first gray spots appear, use one of the appliances below to create a movement of air. This gives a bed of coals in 5 to 10 minutes. We suggest using this method only in an emergency.

Hand operated bellows
Electric hair dryer
Electric fan or vacuum
Battery operated blower

Never do this after your meat is on the spit or grill, the ash will blow all over the food and ruin it.

foil drip pans

meat to buy

how to make drip pans

Catch fats and juices for making gravies or sauces to serve with the meat.

Take an 18″ roll of heavy duty aluminum foil. Tear off two sheets, each about 5″ longer than the meat to be barbecued. Lay one sheet on top of the other.

Fold foil in half lengthwise. Now you have four thicknesses of foil, 9″ wide and 5″ longer than the meat.

Form the sides and ends 1½″ high. Use a board or paper board box to make a neat square fold. Pull out the corners from the sides as shown.

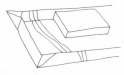

Fold the corners back against the sides. This leaves the inside seams tight and smooth, so drippings will not leak out.

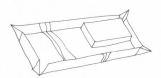

The finished tray is about 6″ wide, has sides 1½″ high. The 4 corners are square and leakproof. The drip pan is now ready to place under the meat.

how to place drip pans

Place the aluminum foil drip pan parallel to and slightly forward of the spit rod in all spit barbecuing. Make sure the drip pan does not rest on the burning briquets. The drip pan catches fats and juices for gravies and is a handy container for liquids used to baste the meats. For indirect covered or Old Fashioned Smoke Cooking place drip pan on fire base under meat.

how to select meat

Meat for a barbecue should be choice meat, such as you would select for roasting or broiling. Only an expert can judge quality by appearance, so it's better to rely on your local meat dealer.

BEEF: Top quality beef is dull red, marbled with streaks of fat throughout the lean, with an outer coating of firm, white fat.

STANDING RIB ROAST: There are usually 7 ribs in the rib section of beef. Never buy less than a 2-rib roast, which will serve 4. With each additional rib you can serve 2 more people. For best results have short ribs cut off and the flank turned over and tied (see page 33).

ROLLED RIB ROAST: This is a rib roast, boned, rolled and tied. Ask the meat dealer to roll the beef around a piece of fat, and to roll extra fat around the outside, before tying. Never buy less than a 4-pound rolled roast, which will serve 4 people.

PORTERHOUSE OR T-BONE STEAK: These are tender and flavorful, but not as easy to carve for a crowd as sirloin. Use steaks from 1½″ to 2″ thick.

SIRLOIN STEAK: Buy a steak from the round end, called the wedge-bone sirloin, for a crowd. Select a steak from 1½″ to 2″ thick.

CLUB STEAK (Delmonico or Shell Steak): These are small steaks with little or no bone. The average 1½″ club steak weighs about 1¼ pounds.

FILLET OF BEEF (Tenderloin): This is always tender and easy to carve. A whole tenderloin weighs from 4 to 10 pounds.

HAMBURGER: Buy lean ground beef, or boned chuck and have it ground.

HAM: Buy a fine, mild-cured, ready-to-eat ham for a barbecue. It will take 1½ to 2 hours on the spit to barbecue a ready-to-eat ham.

LEG OF LAMB: This roast usually weighs 6 to 8 pounds. Spring lamb is best and usually can be purchased all year long.

CHICKEN: For whole or halved broilers, your best buy is meaty, tender, ready-to-cook birds that can be bought fresh or ice-chilled, or quick-frozen in a package. Never buy hens for barbecuing. Chicken may also be purchased in parts. The breasts, drumsticks, thighs, and possibly wings, are suitable for the barbecue.

TURKEY: Again, your best buy is the ready-to-cook bird. Today, turkeys are available in many sizes, from the broiler-fryers (3 to 4 pounds) and small roasters (5 to 8 pounds), to the larger young hen (12 to 16 pounds) or tom turkeys (18 to 30 pounds) ready-to-cook weight.

DUCKLING: Buy ready-to-cook ducklings, weighing 5 to 6 pounds.

LOBSTER: The most desirable lobsters weigh from 1 to 2 pounds each. Be sure they are alive when purchased. Split the lobsters yourself or, ask the dealer to split and clean them for you.

how much meat to buy

Outdoor appetites are healthy appetites and the ordinary recommendations as to how much meat to buy, per person, are apt to be on the skimpy side. For a barbecue feast it is better to err on the side of abundance than to let anyone go hungry.

The cut of meat and preparation of it by the meat man influence the amount you buy. When purchasing meat with bone in, such as standing rib roast of beef, leg of lamb or porterhouse steak, you'd better count on from ¾ to one pound per person. If the meat has no bone or has been boned (hamburg, top sirloin for shish kabobs and rolled roast of beef), then from ⅓ to ½ pound per person is generally sufficient.

Use the following suggestions as a general guide:

BEEF: In purchasing porterhouse and sirloin steaks, have them cut about 1½" thick. If the menu calls for club or rib steaks, allow 1 steak per person and they should be at least 1½" thick.

Never barbecue less than a 2-rib roast or a 4-pound rolled rib roast. Fillets of beef weigh from 4 to 10 pounds. Half of a 4-pound fillet is the smallest piece you can satisfactorily barbecue.

PORK: Buy two 1-inch rib pork chops per person or 1 to 1½ center-cut chops. Allow about 1 pound of barbecued spareribs per person. You can barbecue a whole pork loin weighing up to 10 pounds or a part of one.

Barbecue at least a half a ham if it has the bone in. You can get a piece with the bone in suitable for barbecuing which weighs as little as 6 pounds; if it's boned use a 4 to 5-pound piece.

LAMB: When serving lamb chops, buy 1 or 2 for each guest depending on whether they are 2" or 1½" thick. Never barbecue less than half a leg of lamb. Have steaks cut from the leg, 1" thick and allow 1 steak per person.

POULTRY: The rule for broilers is a half per person. For whole chicken or turkey allow ¾ of a pound per person. For chicken parts, barbecue a whole breast, 2 to 3 drumsticks or 2 thighs per person. Rock Cornish game hens vary in size. Their weights range from 12 ounces to 3 pounds. So, follow the rule of one small hen (14 to 16 ounces) per person, or a half or quarter of a larger one. For duckling allow ½ per person.

FISH AND SEAFOOD: For fish fare, allow 1 whole small fish such as rainbow trout or about ½ pound of a large fish for each guest.

You'll want one small lobster or half a large one per guest or 1 pound of rock lobster tails and when shrimp is the dish, have on hand ½ pound (uncooked) per guest.

how to use a spit

standing rib roast of beef

Step 1. As shown in Fig. 1, have meat sawed through backbone to free ribs. Insert suet in cut area. Saw through ribs about 2½ inches from ends; remove small bones. Leave meat attached to form a flap; fold over bone ends. Tie roast at 1-inch intervals with heavy twine (Fig. 2).

Step 2. Slip a spit fork on rod. Insert point of rod through thickest part of meat (Fig. 2). Put second fork on rod; insert both into meat. Center meat on rod. Tighten fork screws slightly.

Step 3. Test large pieces of meat and poultry for balance by rotating spit rod on palms of hands (Fig. 3). Tighten fork screws with pliers.

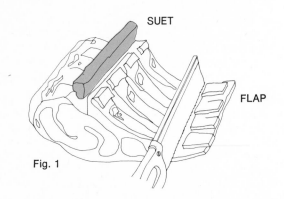

SUET

FLAP

Fig. 1

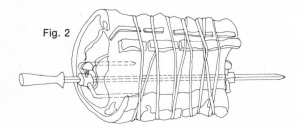

Fig. 2

pork loin

Cut a pork loin into 3 equal pieces, see page 40 or leave whole. Following Step 2 above, arrange meat on rod with a spit fork at both ends of each piece. Test for balance, see Step 3 above.

ham

Have ham cut in half diagonally (Fig. 4). Put a spit fork on rod. Run rod through ham, offsetting butt end for better balance. Put second fork on rod and insert forks in ham; if necessary, use a hammer. Test for balance, see Step 3 above. Center meat. Tighten screws.

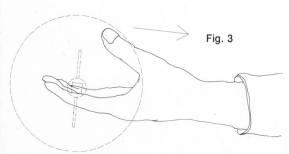

Fig. 3

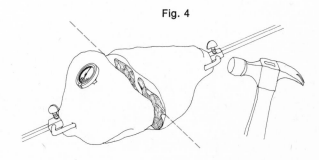

Fig. 4

leg of lamb

Have 3 inches of bone sawed from small end of leg. Leave meat around bone intact to form a flap. Put a spit fork on rod. Fold flap up and run rod through flap and leg (Fig. 5). Put second fork on rod and insert one in each end of leg. Test for balance. See Step 3, page 16. Tighten screws.

Fig. 8

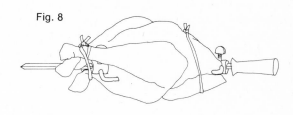

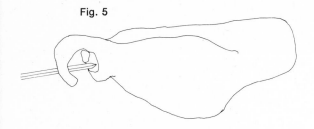

Fig. 5

turkey

Step 1. Lay turkey breast side down. Bring neck skin up over neck cavity. Turn under edges of skin; skewer to back skin (Fig. 6). Loop twine around skewer and tie. Turn breast side up. Tie or skewer wings to body (Fig. 7).

Step 2. Put a spit fork on rod. Insert rod in neck skin parallel to backbone; bring it out just above tail. Put a second fork on rod. Insert forks in breast and tail areas (Fig. 8). Test for balance. See Step 3, page 16. Tighten screws with pliers. Tie tail to rod with twine. Cross legs; tie to tail. Tying makes bird more compact and holds it more securely on the rod.

single chicken on a spit

To prepare a single chicken for spit barbecuing, follow Steps 1 and 2 for Turkey, above. Be sure chicken is centered on rod.

three chickens on a spit

Tie or skewer wings to bodies. Put a spit fork on rod. Dovetail chickens on rod. Loop twine around tails and legs; tie to rod. Put second fork on rod; insert forks in end chickens. Tighten screws with pliers (see Fig. 9).

Fig. 9

Fig. 6

Fig. 7

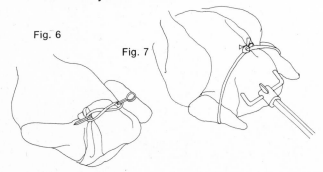

how to use a thermometer

barbecue to perfection

There are several ways to determine when a roast or large piece of meat is done, but the really accurate way is to use a barbecue thermometer. The sturdy pointed metal end or tip will never break off and always gives an accurate reading. Insert the barbecue thermometer at an angle so the pointed end rests in the center of the thickest part of the meat. Be careful that it doesn't touch the spit or the bone and that the point is not resting in fat, or you will get a false reading.

Leave the thermometer in place while the meat revolves. Reduce the fire just before the desired temperature is reached. The meat will continue to cook. When the pointer reaches the proper place on the dial, the meat is done. Remove the thermometer and take the meat off the spit.

HAM: Fig. 3 and picture on page 37 show the thermometer inserted in the middle of the heaviest section of the ham.

Fig. 3

OTHER MEATS: For placement of thermometer, see Standing Rib Roast of Beef page 33, Leg of Lamb page 41 and Pork Loin page 40 (see Fig. 4).

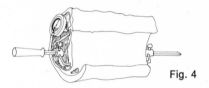

Fig. 4

the right way

POULTRY: Insert tip of thermometer in thick part of thigh close to the body or in heavy part of breast; see Fig. 1, Turkey recipe page 29; Chicken recipe page 27.

Fig. 1

ROLLED ROAST: As shown in Fig. 2, insert thermometer so tip is in center of the roast. Take care the tip does not touch the spit.

Fig. 2

the wrong way

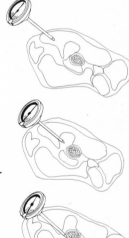

Too near the surface— not in center of meat— reading will be high.

Pointed end rests in fat— reading will be low.

End of the thermometer touches bone— reading will be high.

Pointed end of thermometer touches spit— reading will be high.

old fashioned covered cooking

smoking for flavor and succulent meats

In the romantic past, when the landed gentry prided themselves on well-stocked larders, the smokehouse was an asset no one could be without. Hams, bacon and other meat hung in the aromatic smoke, taking on delectable flavor, until properly cured. Today, with the Big Boy Barrel circulating, controlled heat you are able to enjoy true old fashioned smoke flavor and at the same time preserve the rich, succulent, natural juices of the meat. This is a real treat you will want to enjoy often. Use chips or small pieces of wood made from fruit and nut woods such as hickory, walnut, cherry and apple. Smoking foods is fun and the rich aroma generates big appetites. Ham, bacon, sausage, spareribs, poultry and fish can be smoked to perfection.

Soak chips or small pieces of wood in water for about 20 minutes. Arrange fire as directed on page 10 and place drip pan in position. Put some soaked chips on briquets as shown in Fig. 1. Place meat on grill or spit as desired and close hood. If you are using the spit turn on motor. After meat starts cooking, add soaked chips or pieces of wood. You control the amount of smoke flavor by the amount of chips you add during barbecuing (do not add too large a quantity at any one time) and by the length of time you cook.

covered country cooking

The advantages and benefits of a Big Boy Barrel are not limited to smoke cooking. These units give circulating, controlled heat perfect for broiling, searing, roasting or grilling. For larger or heavier meats such as roasts use indirect method with fire at both ends of grill as shown in Fig. 1. For smaller pieces of meat use direct method as shown in Fig. 2.

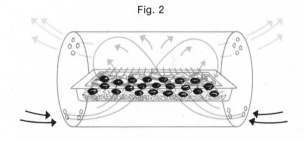

Fig. 2

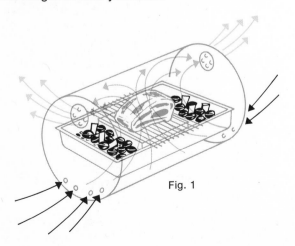

Fig. 1

On units with the built-in electric element an entirely new unique method of barbecuing is possible. This new two-way barbecuing method uses both infrared heat from the electric element and the flavorful radiated heat of the charcoal. After starting the fire use the heat of the electric element to sear in juices of meat during the first five minutes. This unit can also be used for supplemental heat during the latter part of barbecuing.

barbecue sauces

Good sauces have great importance in barbecuing certain meats. So, why not become an expert on the making of sauces. We prefer a sauce that enhances the meat flavor but does not overpower it. The recipes on page 21 are among our top favorites, but you may have one that you prefer above all others. If so, by all means continue to use it. If not, try one of ours as a guide, altering it to suit your own taste.

Even more important than the recipes are the rules for using them. When barbecuing roasts or poultry on the spit, we personally prefer to apply the sauce generously during the last few minutes of the barbecuing period. Besides adding flavor, it keeps the meat moist and appetizing. When applied in this way, you taste the sauce and the meat separately. If you baste constantly while barbecuing, you taste only the condiments in the sauce—the meat flavor will lose its identity. In addition, if the sauce has tomato as an ingredient, it will burn and char long before the meat is cooked.

Marinades are used on meats before barbecuing to give flavor and sometimes to tenderize them. Try a marinade for such meats as steaks, lamb chops and other small cuts. To marinate meat, cover it with the prepared mixture and chill in the refrigerator for several hours; turn several times to allow the flavor to penetrate more evenly. If you prefer a stronger flavor, refrigerate overnight. After draining meat be sure to let it come to room temperature before barbecuing or timing will be off.

You can save any leftover marinade to use another time. Store it in a tightly covered jar in refrigerator.

A glaze for barbecued ham, such as our Pineapple Glaze, makes it beautiful as well as flavorful.

Recipes on page 21 are ones we used in barbecuing the meats pictured in this book. Try them, then make your own special variations.

barbecue sauce

2 bottles (14 ounces each) ketchup
1 bottle (12 ounces) chili sauce
⅓ cup prepared mustard
1 tablespoon dry mustard
1½ cups firmly packed brown sugar
2 tablespoons coarse, freshly ground
   black pepper
1½ cups wine vinegar
1 cup fresh lemon juice
½ cup bottled thick steak sauce
Dash Tabasco, or to taste
¼ cup Worcestershire sauce
1 tablespoon soy sauce
2 tablespoons salad oil
1 can (12 ounces) beer
Minced or crushed garlic, if desired

Combine all ingredients except the garlic and mix well. Pour into pint jars to store. This sauce may be stored for several weeks in the refrigerator. For longer storage, freeze in freezer. About an hour before using the sauce, add the garlic if desired. Makes about 6 pints.

basting sauce

½ cup cooking oil
¾ cup wine vinegar
¼ cup water
2 teaspoons salt
3 tablespoons sugar
1½ teaspoons Tabasco sauce
¼ teaspoon Worcestershire sauce
1 small bay leaf

Combine all ingredients in a small saucepan. Bring to a boil over medium heat. Keep warm by the side of the fire while using. Makes about 1½ cups sauce.

glossy cherry sauce

1 can (1 pound) unsweetened cherries
Water
1 tablespoon cornstarch
2 tablespoons melted butter
¼ cup lemon juice
1 teaspoon grated lemon peel
⅛ teaspoon salt
½ teaspoon cinnamon
¼ cup sugar
Few drops red food coloring, if desired

Drain cherries and measure juice. Set cherries aside. Add enough water to cherry juice to make 1½ cups liquid. Blend ¼ cup of the liquid with cornstarch in a small bowl.

In a saucepan, combine all the ingredients except cherries. Bring mixture to a boil; slowly add and stir in reserved cornstarch mixture. Cook and stir sauce until thickened. Add cherries; simmer about 5 minutes, stirring occasionally. Stir in food coloring. Serve sauce hot. Makes about 2½ cups.

onion sauce

1 tablespoon butter or margarine
2 tablespoons sugar
2 medium-size onions, sliced
1 tablespoon flour
2 beef bouillon cubes
1 cup boiling water
1 tablespoon vinegar
Salt, to taste

Melt butter in a skillet; stir in sugar. Separate onion slices into rings and put in melted butter. Cook onion over low heat, stirring often, until almost tender but not brown. Remove from heat. Sprinkle flour over onions and toss gently to moisten. Dissolve bouillon cubes in boiling water and slowly add and stir into onion mixture. Return sauce to medium heat; bring to a boil, stirring constantly. Reduce heat to low; cook and stir until sauce is slightly thickened and smooth or, about 5 minutes. Add and stir in vinegar and salt; serve hot. Makes about 2 cups sauce.

marinade

1½ cups salad oil
¾ cup soy sauce
¼ cup Worcestershire sauce
2 tablespoons dry mustard
2¼ teaspoons salt
1 tablespoon coarse, freshly ground
   black pepper
½ cup wine vinegar
1½ teaspoons dried parsley flakes
2 crushed garlic cloves, if desired
⅓ cup fresh lemon juice

Combine all ingredients and mix well. Make about 3½ cups. Marinade can be drained from steaks or chops for a second use. Store in a tightly covered jar in freezer indefinitely, or in refrigerator for 1 week.

easy basting sauce

Combine ⅓ cup wine vinegar, ⅓ cup fresh lemon juice and ⅓ cup salad oil. Add ½ teaspoon soy sauce and coarse, freshly ground black pepper and salt to taste. Mix well. Makes 1 cup.

honey-clove glaze

Combine ½ cup honey, ¼ cup lemon juice, ½ teaspoon ground cloves and 2 teaspoons soy sauce in a small, screw-top jar. Stir to mix well. Heat just before using. Makes ⅔ cup.

pineapple glaze

1 can (8 ounces) crushed pineapple
1 cup firmly packed brown sugar
1 tablespoon prepared mustard
1 teaspoon dry mustard
Juice of 1 lemon
Dash of salt

Drain syrup from pineapple and reserve. Combine drained pineapple and remaining ingredients in a blender; blend until smooth. Add as much of the reserved syrup as necessary to have the mixture of good spreading consistency. Brush over meat during the last few minutes of barbecuing. Makes about 1½ cups.

steaks, the barbecue favorite

how do you like your steaks?

Everyone likes steak, the question is how do they like it cooked? Some connoisseurs, self-appointed or elected, shudder at the thought of cooking steak beyond the rare stage. Frankly that's our choice, for we like steak with a "just cooked" flavor and good red color. But each to his own taste we say. So cook steaks the way you and your guests like them.

Steak is the favorite food of Americans of all ages, both male and female, and has been ever since the first prime steer came off the mid-west ranches. And barbecuing is certainly the preferred way to prepare steaks.

here is how they should look:

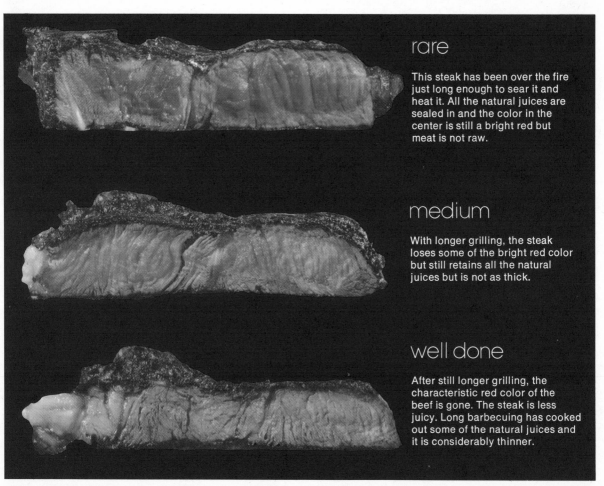

rare

This steak has been over the fire just long enough to sear it and heat it. All the natural juices are sealed in and the color in the center is still a bright red but meat is not raw.

medium

With longer grilling, the steak loses some of the bright red color but still retains all the natural juices but is not as thick.

well done

After still longer grilling, the characteristic red color of the beef is gone. The steak is less juicy. Long barbecuing has cooked out some of the natural juices and it is considerably thinner.

Barbecuing for a crowd? One, two or three huge steaks fit on the brazier with room to spare. You'll know it's time to turn the steaks when droplets of bright red juices rise on the uncooked side. Turn them just once to save the juices.

steak memos from big boy

Remove steaks from the refrigerator or freezer long enough ahead of time so that they will reach room temperature before they are put on the grill. This makes it easier to estimate barbecuing time.

Rub grill with cooking oil or the fat edge of the steak to lubricate the grill and reduce sticking and make for easier clean-up.

Turn a steak only once. Always use tongs for turning. Never use a fork which pierces the meat and lets juices escape. To prevent steak from curling, score or slit the fat on the edges at about 1½" intervals before placing it on the grill. Be careful not to cut the meat or you will lose precious juices. It is not necessary to score steaks that are 1½" or thicker.

We prefer to season our steaks, except marinated ones, after barbecuing with salt and coarse, freshly ground black pepper. However, some folks like to season the barbecued side of steak immediately after it is turned and complete seasoning the second side when barbecuing is done. You can pound cracked peppercorns into top and bottom surface of steak before barbecuing. Salt draws out the juices so it is best to salt to your taste when the steak is on your plate. Marinated steaks do not require seasoning after barbecuing.

For garlic-flavored steak, rub both sides of the steak with a cut clove of garlic before barbecuing.

The time to turn the steak is when droplets of bright red juices rise on the uncooked side.

to barbecue steak properly

Keep flame-ups and smoke to a minimum yet use a hot (**MEDIUM** to **MEDIUM-HIGH**) heat. If the juices are sputtering and flaming excessively reduce the heat.

FOR CHARCOAL GRILLED STEAKS: Give careful attention to arranging the briquets. After they are coated with gray ash, spread them out on the gravel or fire base ½" to ¾" apart and knock off the gray ash. If, in spite of these precautions, you do have flame-up, raise the grill or lower the fire box for a few minutes. If you have the fire arranged the way we recommend and you do get a little flame-up, don't worry about it. You may sear the steak too well or char it a little, but most people like it this way anyhow.

FOR GAS GRILLED STEAKS: Remove grill and preheat ceramic rocks on **HIGH** for about 3 minutes. Oil grill and sear steaks as directed in recipe. Barbecue on **MEDIUM** heat and if there is excessive flame-up rotate grill ¼ turn or reduce heat.

sirloin steaks for a crowd

Allow ¾ to 1 pound of steak per person. Buy sirloin of beef from 1½ to 2 inches thick. When 2 inches thick, it is much easier to slice for sandwiches. Fresh or frozen, it should be at room temperature before barbecuing.

Rub the fat edge across the grill as an oiled grill prevents the steak from sticking.

FOR CHARCOAL GRILLING: Arrange the fire as indicated on page 11. Knock the gray ash off the briquets. Adjust the grill or fire box so the briquets are about 3 inches below the grill (**HIGH** heat). Arrange steaks on the grill and sear 2 or 3 minutes. Then lower the fire box or raise the grill so the briquets are about 5 or 6 inches below the meat (**MEDIUM** heat). When the juices come to the surface, the steak is ready to turn. Turn the steak and with the briquets about 3 inches below the steaks sear for 2 or 3 minutes. Position grill or fire box so briquets are 5 to 6 inches below the meat and complete barbecuing.*

FOR GAS GRILLING: Preheat the brazier on **HIGH** for about 3 minutes. Arrange steak on the grill and turn heat to **HIGH** and sear for about 2 minutes. Then turn heat to **MEDIUM** and continue barbecuing. When the juices come to the surface, the steak is ready to turn. Turn the steak. Turn heat to **HIGH** and sear second side about 1 or 2 minutes. Then turn back to **MEDIUM** and continue to barbecue.*

*Turn the steak using tongs or a spatula, never spear a steak with a fork. To barbecue steak 2 inches thick to the rare stage, it takes 10 to 15 minutes total searing and barbecuing time for each side. Do not use too high a heat. Allow a slightly longer time for medium and well-done steak. To determine whether steak is done as desired, use a small sharp knife and make a slit alongside the bone. Sprinkle with salt and coarse, freshly ground black pepper and serve at once, plain or with Barbecue Sauce (see page 21).

Sirloin steak sliced at an angle across the grain in thin slices is a crowd pleaser. This method permits the chef to enjoy hot barbecued steak sandwiches with the crowd.

Club steaks, small and with little or no bone, are perfect for individual servings. Barbecuing these tender, mouth-watering triangles of meat is so easy. Don't let flavorful juices escape by trying to turn steak with a fork— use a good pair of tongs.

char-grilled club steaks

Allow 1 club steak for each person and have them cut at least 1½ inches thick. Marinate the steak several hours in Marinade (see page 21) in the refrigerator. Then bring to room temperature. Rub grill with oil or a piece of fat. Drain excess Marinade from steaks and lay them on the grill.

FOR CHARCOAL GRILLING: Space briquets ½ to ¾ inch apart. Adjust grill so briquets are about 3 inches below the steaks. Sear 2 or 3 minutes and then adjust grill so briquets are about 5 or 6 inches below steaks. Continue to barbecue until juices appear on the top surface. Turn steaks with tongs and adjust grill so briquets are about 3 inches below the steaks. Sear steaks for 2 or 3 minutes then adjust grill so briquets are about 5 or 6 inches below steaks. Continue to barbecue until done.*

FOR GAS GRILLING: Preheat the brazier on **HIGH** for about 3 minutes. Arrange steaks on grill, turn heat to **HIGH** and sear steaks about 2 minutes. Turn heat to **MEDIUM** and continue to barbecue until juices appear on the top surface. Turn steaks with tongs and turn heat to **HIGH** and sear them for about 1 minute. Turn heat to **MEDIUM** and continue to barbecue until done. Allow 6 to 8 minutes total searing and barbecuing time for each side. Remove meat from grill and serve at once.*

*Allow 6 to 8 minutes total searing and barbecuing time for each side. Remove meat from the grill and serve at once.

If time doesn't permit marinating steaks they are excellent barbecued plain. Marinated steaks do not require seasoning so you must add seasoning to plain steaks when you take them off grill.

Tenderest of all beef cuts, the tenderloin (fillet of beef) rotating slowly over hot flame until it is crisp and brown outside, deep pink and juicy within is something special indeed! Thicker at one end than the other, it just cooks rare, medium and well-done all in one simple operation dissolving all steak problems for the host.

rare   medium   well done

barbecued beef tenderloin

Lower quality tenderloins are best for barbecuing because they have the least fat. A beef tenderloin strip weighs from 4 to 8 pounds. Allow ⅓ to ½ pound meat per person. Have the meat at room temperature. Trim all excess fat off the meat or it will slow down the cooking. Either cut off the narrow tip of meat or fold it over and tie or skewer it in place to prevent its charring. With a spit fork on rod, run the spit rod through the center of meat; put a second fork on rod and put spit forks into the ends of the meat and tighten fork screws.

FOR CHARCOAL BARBECUING: Arrange briquets at the rear of the spit. Be sure the fire's hot. The extreme tenderness and lack of fat makes it important to barbecue a tenderloin quickly over a very hot fire. Place the drip pan in front of briquets and under the spit as shown. Attach the spit and start the motor.*

FOR GAS BARBECUING: Attach the spit and start the motor. Light gas and set at **MEDIUM** to **MEDIUM-HIGH**.*

*Tenderloin, because it is not one of the juiciest cuts, should always be cooked so that the thickest portion is still pink in color. Otherwise, meat will be dry. To tell when meat is done, make a deep slit in the thickest portion with a sharp knife and note the color, or use a thermometer. Thermometer should read 140°. This takes about 30 to 45 minutes. Remove the meat from the spit. Sprinkle with salt. Cut in crosswise slices to serve. Leftovers can be frozen.

If meat is done before serving time, lower the fire box to the lowest position or turn to **LOW** to keep the meat hot without further cooking. It cooks only when juices bubble on the surface.

chickens on the spit

Use whole, ready-to-cook broiler-fryers weighing from 2 to 3½ pounds each. Allow ½ chicken per person. Buy chickens uniform in weight when barbecuing more than one so that they'll all be cooked at the same time. Sprinkle the body cavities of each chicken with 1 teaspoon salt.

See directions on page 17, to arrange chickens on the spit. If you choose to take a short cut, do not tie the wings. As the chickens cook, the heat will draw the wings up against the bodies. Tighten fork screws. Brush the outsides of chickens with oil. Insert barbecue thermometer in thickest part of thigh of the center chicken (see page 18).

FOR CHARCOAL BARBECUING: Heap the briquets slightly at the rear of the fire box. Make sure they cover an area slightly longer than the chickens on the spit. Otherwise, the end chickens will not cook as quickly as the center one.

Now place the drip pan in front of the briquets as pictured. For 3 chickens, it should be as long as the fire box. Attach the spit and start the motor.*

FOR GAS BARBECUING: Light the gas. Set heat at **MEDIUM** attach the spit and start the motor. Be sure the fire is hot enough to brown the chickens but not so hot it blisters the skin. Chickens are cooking when juices come to the surface and bubble.*

*Chickens are done when the thermometer registers 190°F. Allow 1½ to 2 hours for 3½ pound chickens, 1 to 1¼ hours for smaller chickens. The meat will have pulled away from the bones, especially at the ends of the legs when cooked.

Constant turning of the chickens makes continual basting unnecessary. For covered units the chicken cooks slightly faster and increases the charcoal flavor, but the skin won't be quite as crisp as it is on a brazier or when the cover is left open.

Bubbling juices on the surfaces of the chickens during barbecuing assures you that the heat is right.

Constant self-basting of the chickens, which you have only in spit barbecuing, makes chicken succulent, tender and brown.

chicken halves in the spit basket

Four chicken halves fit perfectly in the spit basket. Use 2 broilers weighing about 3 pounds each. Have the meat man split them and break the joints so the broilers will be as flat as possible. Rub skin sides and spit basket with oil. This prevents the skin from sticking to the basket during cooking.

Run the spit rod through the spit basket brackets and lay the broilers in it, skin-side up, so the legs are toward the ends as shown. Put the basket cover in place but do not clamp it down too tightly. Tighten thumb screws.

FOR CHARCOAL BARBECUING: Heap the briquets slightly at the rear of the fire box. Place the aluminum foil drip pan in front of the briquets.

Attach the spit and start the motor. Keep the fire box at the highest position until chickens are seared, taking care not to blister the skin. Then reduce heat by lowering the fire box 6″ to 7″ from the chickens, but be sure that barbecuing continues.*

FOR GAS BARBECUING: Light the gas. Set heat at **MEDIUM** attach the spit and start the motor.*

*Juices on the surface should continue to bubble as the spit revolves. The constant turning of the chicken keeps them self-basted so that basting while barbecuing is unnecessary.

Stop the spit three times, at well-spaced intervals, with the cut sides of the chicken toward the heat and do not start it again for 15 to 30 seconds. These periods of concentrated heat sear the chicken and seal in the juices.

During the last 10 minutes, baste the chicken with Barbecue Sauce or Pineapple Glaze (see page 21). The total barbecuing time will be about 1 to 1¼ hours. When chicken is fork-tender, remove from the spit basket to a hot platter and serve immediately. Leftovers can be frozen.

turkey on the spit

What is more appetizing than a big 16 to 18 pound Tom Turkey turning a golden brown as it turns on the spit? This is the best way to be sure the turkey is well cooked, yet retains its succulent juices.

Select a ready-to-cook, plump, fresh or quick-frozen turkey. Allow ¾ pound of turkey per person. If frozen, thaw it completely or it will be difficult to estimate barbecuing time. Wash inside and outside of turkey well and remove any remaining bits of lung and liver from the cavity.

For added flavor, rinse the inside with wine vinegar. For a 15 to 20 pound bird, put about 2 tablespoons salt in the body cavity and about 1 or 2 tablespoons more salt in the neck cavity. Allow a total of about 1 tablespoon salt for each 4 pounds of turkey. For additional flavor, mix the salt with coarse, fresh ground black pepper and cooking oil to make a paste which you then spread in the cavities.

Secure neck skin; tie or skewer wings and put turkey on spit rod as directed on page 17 and test for balance. Insert meat thermometer tip in the thickest part of the thigh, close to the body or if you stuff the bird, place the tip in the center of the stuffing.

FOR CHARCOAL BARBECUING: Heap briquets at the back of the fire bowl or box. Place drip pan in front of briquets. Brush turkey with cooking oil or rub with butter. Attach spit and sear turkey about 2 minutes taking care the skin does not blister. Arrange fire or lower fire box so turkey continues to cook.*

FOR GAS BARBECUING: Remove grill, turn control to **HIGH** and light the brazier. Turn heat to **MEDIUM**. Brush turkey with cooking oil or rub with butter. Attach spit and turn on motor. Turn heat to **HIGH** for about 2 minutes to sear turkey. Return heat to **MEDIUM**. Be sure the skin does not blister as juices will be lost and turkey will be dry.*

*Keep the heat just high enough so that juices continue to come to the surface of the turkey and bubble.

Allow a total of 12 to 15 minutes per pound barbecuing time, but watch the thermometer. During the last 10 minutes of barbecuing, baste turkey with drippings or use melted butter or margarine. When turkey is done thermometer should read 190°. Remove thermometer and spit rod and let turkey stand 10 minutes to firm up.

chicken on the grill

It is true economy and your guests will be happier if you buy chicken parts rather than cut-up whole chickens when you are barbecuing for a crowd. No one wants the backs or the other bony parts.

Brush the grill and chicken parts with cooking oil. Arrange chicken parts on grill with skin side up.

FOR CHARCOAL GRILLING: Space briquets over the gravel, allowing at least ½ inch between each one. Too many briquets will cause chicken to burn before cooking. Start barbecuing chicken with the skin-side up. With the briquets about three inches from the grill sear the chicken for 3 or 4 minutes. Turn chicken parts and baste with Easy Basting Sauce (see page 21) or melted butter or margarine and sear for 3 or 4 minutes. Adjust the grill so briquets are about 6 inches below the chicken. Continue to turn every 6 or 8 minutes and baste after each turn.*

FOR GAS GRILLING: Light the gas. Set the heat at **MEDIUM** to **MEDIUM-HIGH**. Start barbecuing chicken with the skin-side up. Sear the chicken for 3 or 4 minutes. Turn chicken parts and baste with Easy Basting Sauce (see page 21) or melted butter or margarine and sear for 3 or 4 minutes. Turn heat to **MEDIUM** or **MEDIUM-LOW**. Continue to turn every 6 to 8 minutes and baste after each turn.*

*Total barbecuing time will be 45 to 60 minutes (see page 13). The chicken is done when the meat pulls away from the bone.

Motorized units are perfect for using the spit basket for chicken parts. Follow the same basic directions as given for Chicken Halves in the Spit Basket (see page 28). Leftovers can be frozen.

grilled tomatoes

Cut 6 medium-size washed and stemmed tomatoes in half crosswise. Melt 3 tablespoons butter or margarine. Brush tomato halves with butter or margarine and mix remaining fat with ½ cup fine dry bread or cereal crumbs and ½ teaspoon each of basil, rosemary and salt. Spoon crumbs over tomatoes. Place to one side of **MEDIUM** grill, 5 to 7 inches above heat until warmed through, 6 to 8 minutes. Yield: 6 servings.

One—two—three—seven! Seven tender, juicy little birds sizzling as they rotate over hot fire makes any barbecue a party. Here's a simple way to double the capacity of your spit rod. Jusk check that you have plenty of extra spit forks—you'll need one to start plus one for each two birds.

rock cornish game hens

Rock Cornish game hens for barbecuing should weigh at least 1 pound. Allow one hen per person. Have the hens at room temperature before barbecuing or cooking time will be longer. Sprinkle ½ teaspoon salt and a little coarse, freshly ground black pepper in body cavity of each bird. Bring neck skin over neck cavity; turn under edges and skewer to back skin. Bring wings forward and flatten against the body between thighs and breast of the bird. Loop twine around wings and neck end several times to secure. Tie legs together.

Put a spit fork on rod. Run rod, crosswise, through lower part of breasts alternating heads and tails. Use one spit fork for each two birds. Add an additional fork to secure the last bird. Rub birds with cooking oil.

FOR CHARCOAL BARBECUING: Arrange briquets at the rear of the fire bowl or box. Place the drip pan in front of briquets. Attach the spit; start the motor. Close the cover if you have a barrel unit.*

FOR GAS BARBECUING: Light the fire. Attach the spit; start the motor. Turn heat to **HIGH** and sear birds for about 2 minutes. Turn heat down to **MEDIUM** or **MEDIUM-LOW** and continue to barbecue until birds are done.*

*Barbecue hens 45 minutes to 1 hour or until done. Brush them often during barbecuing with Easy Basting Sauce (see page 21). Game hens are done when meat pulls away from the leg bones.

BARBECUED SQUABS: They weigh from ½ to 1 pound each. Allow 1 per person. Follow directions above for tying and putting Cornish Game Hens on rod but place a piece of salt pork over each breastbone securing it while tying wings to body. Barbecue as directed for Cornish Game Hens.

Our heritage from across the seas, the Roast Beef of Old England is still everybody's favorite—men, women and children. So, you'll never go wrong serving a barbecued Standing Rib Roast! We prefer our beef rare or medium with a nicely browned outside, rosy red inside and an abundance of bright red juices.
But, if you prefer yours well done, remember you'll get fewer servings per pound because the roast will not be so plump and full.

barbecued standing rib roast

When buying a rib roast of beef for barbecuing, allow from ¾ to 1 pound of meat per serving but never barbecue less than a 2-rib roast. A smaller roast shrinks too much. Have the meat man prepare the roast as shown on page 16.

Bring the meat to room temperature and put it on the spit rod. Insert the spit forks; tighten the screws and test for balance. Insert the barbecue thermometer in the center of roast. Reading will not be true if tip of thermometer touches the spit or bone, rests in fat or is not centered in meat. (See page 18.)

FOR CHARCOAL BARBECUING: Arrange the ash-coated briquets at the rear of the fire box. Place the drip pan in front (see page 14). Attach the spit and start the motor. Keep the fire box at the highest position, until roast is seared. Lower the fire box 6 to 8 inches from the roast, but be sure that barbecuing continues. Juices should come to the surface and bubble constantly. If a garlic flavor is desired, throw several cloves on the hot briquets.*

FOR GAS BARBECUING: Attach the spit and start the motor. Light the fire and set at **HIGH** heat. Sear the roast for 3 or 4 minutes. Turn the heat to **MEDIUM** or **MEDIUM-LOW** and continue to barbecue until done. For garlic flavor throw several cut up cloves of garlic or garlic salt onto the ceramic rocks.*

*Barbecue until thermometer registers 140° for rare, 160° for medium and 170° for well done. Size of roast and amount of heat as explained on page 13 determine actual barbecuing time. Generally speaking it takes from 12 to 15 minutes per pound to barbecue a roast rare to medium.

When roast is done, lift out thermometer, remove meat from the spit and allow it to stand in a warm place 10 minutes to firm up before carving.

rolled roast beef

Allow about ⅓ to ½ pound of meat per person when serving a rolled rib roast. Never barbecue less than 4 pounds. Smaller roasts shrink more, will not be as juicy, will have no rare center and are more difficult to carve. Have meat man roll meat around a strip of fat and put a covering of fat about ¼ inch thick around the roast before he ties it with heavy twine. This covering of fat helps hold in the juices. Bring meat to room temperature before barbecuing or cooking time will be longer.

Put the roast on the spit as shown. Insert the spit forks and tighten screws. Then test for balance. Insert barbecue thermometer, as shown.

FOR CHARCOAL BARBECUING: Heap the briquets at the rear of the fire box. Put the drip pan in front. Attach the spit and start the motor. If fire becomes too hot during barbecuing, reduce it by lowering the fire box or removing some hot briquets.*

FOR GAS BARBECUING: Attach the spit and start the motor. Light the fire and set at **HIGH** heat. Sear the roast for 3 or 4 minutes. Turn the heat to **MEDIUM** or **MEDIUM-LOW** and continue to barbecue until done.*

*You'll know roast is cooking as long as juices come to the surface and bubble. Juices and fat self-baste the meat making basting unnecessary and keep the twine from burning. Barbecue roast using the thermometer as a guide: 140° for rare, 160° for medium, 170° for well done. Allow about 12 to 15 minutes per pound. When cooked, remove thermometer and take meat off spit. Before carving, let roast stand in a warm place about 10 minutes to firm up and make carving easier. Cut in crosswise slices to serve. Leftovers can be frozen.

As meat cooks, thermometer often works its way slightly up and out of its original position. Before removing meat from heat check that thermometer tip is still at center of meat by gently pressing it into roast. If reading drops, meat is not fully cooked.

four economy beef quickies

savory short ribs

Short ribs are on the bony side and have considerable fat, so allow at least 1 pound per person. Have the meat man cut them in serving-size pieces. Prepare Marinade (recipe on page 21) and pour it over them. Let stand in the refrigerator overnight. Then drain well and reserve the remaining Marinade.

FOR CHARCOAL BARBECUING: Space the briquets over the gravel about ½ to ¾ inch apart. Rub the grill with cooking oil or a piece of fat to prevent ribs from sticking. Place the ribs on the grill about 4 inches above the briquets. Grill slowly 25 to 35 minutes, turning frequently to prevent ribs from drying out.*

FOR GAS BARBECUING: Rub the grill with cooking oil or a piece of fat. Place the ribs on the grill. Light the fire and set at **MEDIUM** or **MEDIUM-LOW**. Grill slowly 25 to 35 minutes, turning frequently to prevent ribs from drying out.*

*During the last 10 minutes, baste several times with more Marinade if you prefer an extra strong flavor. When done, season with salt and black pepper. Serve with Barbecue Sauce (see page 21).

grilled london broil

Flank steak is the cut of meat to use for Grilled London Broil. A flank steak weighs from 1½ to 2½ pounds. When buying, allow about ½ pound per person. To help tenderize it, score the steak lightly, crisscross fashion, on both sides with a very sharp knife.

FOR CHARCOAL BARBECUING: Space the briquets from ½ to ¾ inch apart on the gravel. Rub the grill with cooking oil and lay the steak on top. Grill about 2 inches above briquets, 5 minutes on each side, turning once.*

FOR GAS BARBECUING: Remove grill, light the fire and set at **HIGH** heat. Preheat grill about 3 or 4 minutes. Turn heat to **MEDIUM**, oil grill and place it in position. Lay steak on top of grill. Barbecue about 5 minutes on each side, turning once.*

*Remove from grill. Cutting diagonally, across the grain, in very thin slices makes the meat more tender. Season with melted butter or margarine, salt and black pepper. Serve topped with Grilled Mushrooms (see page 55). Leftovers can be frozen.

beef roly-polies

Allow 2 cube steaks for each person. Pound the steaks with a wooden mallet to flatten them. Spread them with prepared mustard and sprinkle with a little drained sweet pickle relish, or lay on each a candied dill pickle strip. Roll up; fasten with small metal skewers and brush with melted butter.

FOR CHARCOAL BARBECUING: Space the briquets ½ to ¾ inch apart over the gravel. Rub the grill with cooking oil to prevent meat from sticking. Lay the beef rolls on the grill about 2 inches above the briquets and grill about 10 minutes, turning once.*

FOR GAS BARBECUING: Remove grill, light the fire and set at **HIGH** heat. Preheat grill about 3 or 4 minutes. Turn heat to **MEDIUM**, oil grill and place it in position. Lay the beef rolls on the grill barbecue about 5 minutes on each side, turning once.*

*When done, sprinkle with salt and pepper. Leftovers can be frozen.

grilled cube steak sandwiches

When serving cube steaks allow 2 for each person. Heat 1 cup Marinade (recipe on page 21) to a boil. Pour over 8 cubed steaks and let stand about 20 minutes, then drain them well.

FOR CHARCOAL BARBECUING: Space the briquets ½ to ¾ inch apart over the gravel. Rub the grill with cooking oil to prevent meat from sticking. Lay the steaks on the grill about 2 inches above the briquets*

FOR GAS BARBECUING: Remove grill, light the fire and set at **HIGH** heat. Preheat grill about 3 or 4 minutes. Turn heat to **MEDIUM**, oil grill and place it in position. Lay the steaks on the grill and barbecue about 2 minutes, turning once.*

*Sprinkle with salt and black pepper. Serve in hot toasted, buttered hamburger buns, topped with a little Marinade. Leftovers can be frozen.

ham 'n pineapple

Buy a "ready-to-eat" ham slice cut 1½ to 2 inches thick. Allow about ½ pound per serving. Prepare Honey-Clove Glaze, page 21. Cut a fresh, ripe pineapple into slices about 1 inch thick. Do not remove skin or core.

FOR CHARCOAL BARBECUING: Start fire as directed on page 10 and arrange briquets as shown on page 11.*

FOR GAS BARBECUING: Remove grill and preheat brazier and Bar-B-Rocks on **HIGH** about 3 to 5 minutes. Turn heat to **MEDIUM** and replace grill.*

*Rub fat edge of ham across grill to oil the rods. Arrange ham slice on grill and barbecue about 15 to 20 minutes. Turn ham slice and arrange pineapple slices on grill. Be sure fire is hot enough to keep the juices bubbling on the edge and top of the ham slice.

After about 10 minutes turn the pineapple slices. Continue to barbecue ham and pineapple for another 10 to 15 minutes. During this period brush ham and pineapple with Honey-Clove Glaze until ham is covered with a glossy glaze.

Remove ham and pineapple from grill. Cut ham into serving pieces and serve with a half slice of pineapple. Each guest cuts away the pineapple core and skin. Hot baked beans and warm French bread complete the meal.

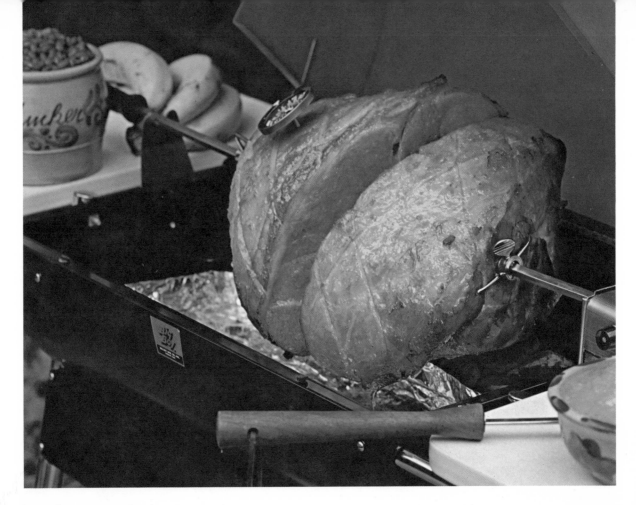

barbecued pineapple glazed ham

Use either a ready-to-eat or uncooked whole ham. Have ham cut in half, diagonally, for better balancing on the spit (see page 17). This also provides greater surface for penetration of the charcoal or smoke flavors. To smoke ham, put a few smoke chips on the briquets during barbecuing (see page 19).

Remove any rind that is left on the ham. Then, score the fat in a diamond pattern. Put ham on the spit as shown on page 17. Insert spit forks at both ends. Center the meat and test for balance. Tighten the screws with pliers. Insert meat thermometer in the center of the thickest section of one half, as shown in photo. Be sure it does not touch the spit or bone or rest in fat.

FOR CHARCOAL BARBECUING: Start the fire as directed on page 10, arrange briquets as shown on page 11, and place drip pan as shown on page 11.*

FOR GAS BARBECUING: Remove grill, turn gas to **HIGH** and light the flame. Turn heat to **MEDIUM.***

*Attach the spit and start the motor. Allow about 10 minutes per pound for a ready-to-eat ham or 25 minutes per pound for an uncooked ham. Baste with Pineapple Glaze (see page 21), during last 15 minutes of barbecuing. When done, meat pulls away from bone. Thermometer should register 140° for a ready-to-eat ham and 170° for an uncooked ham.

PORK CHOPS: A spit basket is best for barbecuing pork chops because they require long slow cooking. Have chops cut about 1 inch thick—and be sure they're uniform in thickness or they'll not all be done at the same time. Run rod through the basket. Arrange chops in the basket and clamp cover over them. Tighten thumb screws on the back of the basket. Spit barbecue chops about 1 hour 10 minutes. Use a small, sharp knife and make a slit alongside the bone to tell when chops are done. The meat should be whitish in color.

barbecued spareribs

Select meaty loin spareribs and allow 1 pound per serving. Allow plenty of time for barbecuing—you will need from 45 minutes to 1 hour. Spareribs like all cuts of pork, require long, slow cooking and must be barbecued to the well-done stage. When done, meat will shrink from the ends of the bones (see photo at right).

For best results, barbecue ribs in a spit basket, or laced on the spit itself. In a spit basket or on a spit, the constant turning bastes the ribs in their own natural juices. For instructions for lacing ribs on the spit, see illustrations on page 39. When barbecuing ribs in the spit basket, slice apart before arranging them in the basket.

FOR CHARCOAL BARBECUING: Arrange the briquets at the rear of the fire box or grill (see page 11). Attach the spit. Place an aluminum foil drip pan in front of the briquets.*

FOR GAS BARBECUING: Remove grill, turn gas to **HIGH** and light the flame. Turn heat to **MEDIUM** and attach the spit.*

*Start the motor. Barbecue until done. If ribs are on the spit, baste them constantly during the last 5 minutes of barbecuing time with Barbecue Sauce (recipe on page 21). When done, slice them apart at once, place individual servings on pieces of aluminum foil and brush generously with Barbecue Sauce. Then wrap and place them in the warming oven or on the edge of the grill to keep warm until serving time.

FOR GRILL BARBECUING: Put the spareribs on the grill with **MEDIUM** heat. During barbecuing, turn them every 2 or 3 minutes and baste at each turn with Basting Sauce (page 21). If this is forgotten, the ribs dry out, burn and lose their rich flavor. When done, cut apart, spread with Barbecue Sauce and wrap in foil, as above.

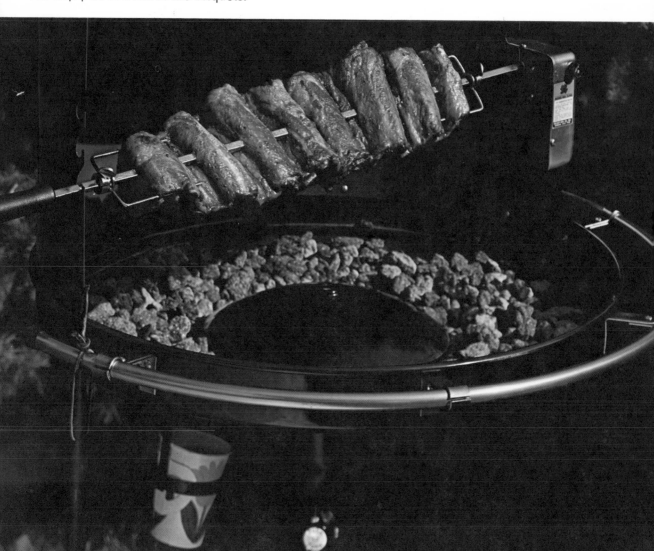

For sheer flavor you cannot beat barbecued spareribs. As they rotate above a hot fire, sizzling in their own rich fat and browning to a turn, their tantalizing fragrance makes waiting almost unbearable!

how to put spareribs on the spit

1. Slip one spit fork on the spit rod and turn the screw just enough to keep the fork in place. Beginning with the narrow end of the ribs, run the spit rod through the middle as shown, so that ribs are laced accordion-fashion. Then, push ribs on to the spit fork.

2. Next, start with the wide end of the second rack of ribs and lace it on the spit rod the same as the first rack. Repeat until all ribs are on the spit, starting first with the narrow end of a rack and following with the wide end. Alternating the racks in this way maintains balance.

3. Bring all ribs to the center of the rod and push together as shown. Slip the second spit fork on the rod; tighten screws on both forks with pliers. Run several metal skewers through the ribs, parallel to the spit rod, to hold them securely. Rod is now ready to attach to the motor.

Serve plenty of barbecue sauce with the spareribs for dunking. See page 21 for recipe. The combination is even better if the sauce has been warmed.

Barbecued spareribs are done when the meat pulls away from the bones.

This is an accurate guide for perfectly barbecued spareribs, whether they have been done on the spit, in the spit basket or on the grill. See photo.

Fig. 1

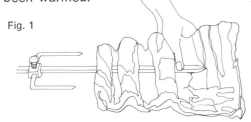

Fig. 2

Fig. 3

hickory smoked pork loin

Once you use a Smoker, your enthusiasm will know no bounds. Everything from domestic poultry and meats to wild fowl and other game, even fish, fresh from sea or stream, takes on an incomparable flavor of hickory to make a barbecue everyone will remember.

When buying a pork loin for barbecuing, allow ¾ to 1 pound per serving, but never barbecue less than a 3½-pound loin. The center cut loin is easier to carve into chop portions but it is usually higher priced than the end roasts. Have meat man split backbone between each rib. Bring pork to room temperature. Put pork on a spit rod as directed on page 17. Insert a meat thermometer in cut end of loin as shown in picture.

For real hickory smoke cooking with tantalizing flavor and aroma, the barrel type unit can't be equalled. To prepare hickory smoke chips see page 19. Or, you may use walnut, apple, or any other fruit wood chips for a delightfully different flavor.

FOR CHARCOAL BARBECUING: Arrange the briquets at the rear of the fire box. Put a drip pan in front of the briquets. Then, lay the smoke chips on top of briquets as directed on page 19. Attach the spit and, with the fire box 5 to 6 inches below the pork loin, start the motor. If you have a covered unit lower the smoker cover.*

FOR GAS BARBECUING: Remove grill, turn gas to **HIGH** and light the flame. Turn heat to **MEDIUM**, attach the spit and start the motor. Sprinkle dampened hickory or orther nut or fruitwood chips onto the Bar-B-Rocks.*

*The smoking time is approximately the same as required for barbecuing, 30 to 35 minutes per pound. But, for the most accurate guide, rely on the thermometer. It should register 190°. When done, the meat will be whitish in color.

If a very heavy smoke flavor is desired, have meat cut in several pieces, use more hickory chips, or allow a slightly longer barbecuing time for smoking. For a longer smoking period, it may be necessary to reduce the heat.

Leftovers can be frozen.

barbecued leg of lamb

Select a 6 to 7-pound leg of lamb and have 3 inches of bone sawed from small end of leg. Leave meat around bone intact to form a flap. Turn the flap of meat up and with a spit fork on the rod, run rod through flap and leg as shown above and on page 17. Press forks into ends of meat. Test for balance and tighten the fork screws.

Rub the entire surface of meat with cooking oil. Then rub with salt and coarse, freshly ground black pepper to season. Insert meat thermometer in the thickest part of the meat as shown above, taking care the tip does not touch the bone, or spit, or rest in fat.

FOR CHARCOAL BARBECUING: Heap the briquets slightly at the back of the fire box or bowl. Set a foil drip pan in front of the briquets (see page 14) and adjust the fire box to about 6 or 7 inches from the meat.*

FOR GAS BARBECUING: Remove grill, turn gas to **HIGH** and light the flame. Turn heat to **MEDIUM.**∗

*Attach the spit and start the motor. If a garlic flavor in the meat is desired, throw a few cloves of garlic or sprinkle garlic salt on the briquets or rocks. Allowing about 30 minutes per pound, barbecue until done. But watch the thermometer and do not remove the lamb until the thermometer registers 180°. During the last 10 minutes of barbecuing, baste with your choice of barbecue sauce. Remove lamb from spit; let stand 10 minutes before carving to firm up.

char-grilled lamb chops

Center-cut loin and rib lamb chops are most suitable for barbecuing. Have them cut from 1 to 2 inches thick and allow about 2 chops per person. You can also grill lamb steaks. Have them cut 1 inch thick and allow 1 per person.

FOR CHARCOAL BARBECUING: When briquets are covered with gray ash space them as directed on page 11. Arrange chops on the grill and lower the grill so it is about 2 inches above the briquets; sear chops 1 to 2 minutes. Then, raise the grill so chops are about 3 inches above briquets. For medium done chops, 1½ inches thick, barbecue about 10 minutes. Lower the grill to 2 inches above briquets; turn chops and sear 1 to 2 minutes on second side. Raise grill again to 3 inches above briquets and continue barbecuing about 10 minutes longer.*

FOR GAS BARBECUING: With grill in position, turn gas to **HIGH**, light flame, lower heat to **LOW**. Arrange chops on oiled grill and turn heat to **HIGH**. Sear chops for 1 to 2 minutes. Then, lower heat to **MEDIUM** and barbecue 1½ inch thick chops about 10 minutes. Turn chops and sear second side on **HIGH** and then continue to barbecue 8 to 10 minutes longer.*

*To tell when meat is cooked, make a slit with a sharp knife alongside the bone. We like our lamb medium done — golden brown outside with just a faint pink tinge inside. For chops about 1 inch thick, allow about 8 minutes on each side for searing and barbecuing. When chops are done, season with salt and coarse, freshly ground black pepper.

barbecued shish kabab

Romance of the Near East in your own back yard! Call them shish-kabab, kebabs, kabobs—what you please—the aroma of well-marinated chunks of tender meat, skewered with bacon and vegetables, turning over a hot fire will bring guests running.

shish kabab and chicken livers

Prepare the appetizer, chicken livers wrapped in bacon, and the main course, shish kabab, together (see photo below). Chicken livers on the grill are smaller and closer to the fire so will cook first.

Follow directions on this page for shish kabab. Wrap chicken livers in one half a strip of bacon and secure with toothpicks. Place hand skewers containing shish kababs in notches in wind-band. Rotate and baste kababs as directed on this page. Arrange chicken livers on the front of the grill. Turn frequently to cook evenly. Bacon should be crisp and liver is cooked when center is gray. Test by making a slit in center of liver.

barbecued shish kabab

There is almost no limit to the variety you can achieve in making shish kabab. The chosen foods can be alternated on one skewer, as shown at right or each type can be strung on a separate skewer.

Beef can be used instead of lamb, strung on the skewer with bacon wrapped around it, and thick slices of celery for a crisp, savory variation.

When barbecuing meats and vegetables together, use smaller pieces of meat than vegetables so everything is done at the same time.

Vegetables alone can be skewered — mushrooms, small whole tomatoes, slices of green peppers and sweet red peppers, quartered onions, sliced zucchini or summer squash.

Marinate the chunks of meat in refrigerator for several hours or longer in a well-seasoned sauce such as Marinade on page 21. Brush kababs with Marinade during the last 5 minutes of barbecuing. When barbecuing vegetables alone, brush with Marinade after they are on the skewers.

A very hot fire is best for Shish Kabab. When using hand skewers, like the one shown at the right, it is necessary to keep rotating them.

Long-handled forks and wire holders make it possible for several kids to "get in the act," toasting marshmallows and barbecuing hot dogs. Note spacing of briquets. Use medium-low heat on gas units.

frankfurter treats

Hot dogs are every bit as versatile as hamburgers, so let the kids try some of these specialties:

DIXIE DOGS: Split frankfurters lengthwise; spread cut surfaces with peanut butter; wrap in a strip of bacon. Barbecue on the grill until bacon is done as desired, turning once. Slide into toasted frankfurter roll.

WISCONSIN'S PRIDE: Split frankfurters lengthwise; insert a thin strip of processed American cheese, wrap in a strip of bacon. Barbecue on the grill until bacon is done as desired, turning once. Slide into toasted frankfurter roll.

BOSTON'S BEST: Split frankfurters lengthwise; spread cut surface with mustard; sprinkle with sweet pickle relish; fill with drained baked beans. Wrap each one securely in a double thickness of heavy duty aluminum foil, twisting the ends. Place on grill and barbecue about 6 to 8 minutes, turning once. Unwrap and serve in toasted frankfurter rolls.

CONEY ISLAND SPECIAL: Split frankfurters lengthwise; spread with mustard; then with ketchup. Fill with drained sauerkraut. Wrap in a double thickness of heavy duty aluminum foil. Place on grill and barbecue 6 to 8 minutes, turning once. Unwrap and serve in a frankfurter roll.

SOUTH-OF-THE-BORDER: Barbecue frankfurters on the grill. Toast split frankfurter rolls on both sides. Arrange 2 halves of toasted rolls on each plate; top with hot chili con carne and 2 sizzling hot frankfurters.

HAMBURGER DOUBLE DECKERS: Make thin hamburger patties, about ¼ inch thick. Put 2 together with any of the following fillings between. Barbecue on the grill about 10 to 12 minutes, turning once. Serve in hamburger buns.

1. A slice of processed American cheese spread with mustard and ketchup.

2. A thin slice of Spanish or Bermuda onion spread with chili sauce and sprinkled with sweet pickle relish.

3. A thin slice of tomato spread with mayonnaise and sprinkled with cut chives or minced onion.

BLUNDERBURGERS: These are featured by a New York hamburger restaurant, which informs the customer that the blunder occurred when the meat was left out!

Toast split hamburger rolls on cut side; spread with mayonnaise. Put together with a slice of cheese, a slice of tomato and half slices of crisp bacon. Barbecue on the grill until cheese melts.

Set out all the "makings" and "trimmings" so that the kids can feast their eyes while they compose their own barbecue masterpieces.

heavenly hamburgers

While hamburgers are very good indeed just cooked plain, the more adventuresome may want to try some innovations, such as the suggestions that follow:

CHEESEBURGERS: Barbecue hamburger on one side. Turn meat and place a slice of processed American cheese on top of each hamburger. When the under side is done, serve in toasted hamburger buns.

knackwurst and bratwurst

Allow about 2 bratwurst or knackwurst per person. Prick each sausage in several places to allow fat to drain during barbecuing and prevent sausages from bursting.

Arrange sausage on the grill, either one variety or both as shown in the photo.

Barbecue knackwurst a total of 10 to 15 minutes and bratwurst a total of 15 to 20 minutes, turning once. During the last few minutes baste with barbecue sauce.

tailgate party

For the kids six through sixty.

A portable unit is great for picnics or the beach.

A barbecue outfit at home will keep the kids in their own backyard busily cooking their favorite foods either for a family meal or for a party of their own. And of course hamburgers and hot dogs are favorite fare. Because they are so popular and easy to prepare, they are frequently served together. Two to three servings to a "customer" is the general rule. One pound of ground beef makes five hamburger patties and there are usually 8 to 9 frankfurters to a pound.

For juicy hamburgers, make thick patties and turn them only once during cooking. Barbecue them 8 to 10 minutes on one side and 5 to 7 minutes after turning. The length of time depends on the factors which influence barbecuing time (see page 13) and on preference for rare, medium or well-done hamburgers.

If frankfurters are scored they won't curl during barbecuing. Franks are precooked and need only to be thoroughly heated and browned.

You can remove some of the hamburgers when rare and continue to barbecue the rest to medium or well-done stage as desired.

Be sure to provide all the additional foods and relishes that make the kids happy; frankfurter and hamburger rolls, sliced onions and tomatoes, crisp lettuce, pickles, pickle relish, mustard, ketchup and other relishes. Mugs of milk are welcome. For dessert, cookies and ice cream, pie, or a luscious fruit shortcake will please everybody (see pages 60 and 61).

Tailgate Party ⟶

barbecued shrimp

Peel and devein 2 pounds of large green (raw) shrimp. Blend ½ cup of butter or margarine with 1 large minced garlic clove, ½ teaspoon of salt, ¼ teaspoon of black pepper and ½ cup of minced parsley. Tear off six 9 " strips of heavy duty aluminum foil. Fold each in half to make a 9" square. Divide shrimp equally on pieces of foil. Top each with 1/6 of butter mixture. Bring foil up around shrimp and twist tightly to seal. Lay foil packages on top of **MEDIUM** grill. Barbecue 5 to 10 minutes or until shrimp is pink and tender. Makes 6 servings.

Barbecued Shrimp

barbecued lobster

Allow 1 small lobster (1 to 1½ pounds) per person. Lobsters must be alive when purchased. You'll know they are really fresh when shells are dark green with red specks. Tails should turn inward and have plenty of spring. They must be split lengthwise and cleaned, with the large claws cracked. Have the fish dealer do this for you, or do it yourself for really fresh lobster.

To clean them yourself, lay the lobster on its back shell on a cutting board. At the place where the tail and body come together, insert the tip of a sharp-pointed knife all the way through to the back shell. With a heavy mallet or hammer, crack the large part of each claw. Then, with a knife, make a cut through the center of the thin undershell from head to tail down through the body, just to the back shell, which should be left intact.

Spread lobster open as far as possible. Lift out and discard the dark vein down the center and the small sac, about 2 inches long, just below the head.

Place lobster on **MEDIUM** grill, shell-side down. Barbecue 15 minutes. Brush lobster generously with melted butter. Sprinkle with salt and pepper. Turn and barbecue 3 to 5 minutes longer. When lobster is done, shell is bright red. Serve with melted butter.

African rock lobster tails are wonderful barbecue fare—they are so easy to cook, to serve and to eat. Peel off the shell and savor the exquisite flavor that is like, yet unlike, our native lobster. One or two of these, with potato salad and hot crispy, French bread, garlic-scented, make a perfect meal.

lobster tail canapés

Allow one lobster tail for each guest. Barbecue according to instructions at right. When done, remove meat from tail in one piece, leaving the shell intact. Cut the meat from each tail into about 6 cubes and put a cocktail pick in each. Pile cubes into the shells. Serve one to each guest with plenty of Barbecue Sauce (page 21) or your favorite cocktail sauce.

char-grilled rock lobster tails

Select frozen rock lobster tails weighing about ½ pound each; allow 2 for each person. Slit tails lengthwise and bend backwards, toward shell side, to crack. This prevents curling during barbecuing and allows butter to penetrate the meat.

ON A CHARCOAL GRILL: Space briquets about ½ to ¾ inch apart over the gravel and on a gas grill set heat at **MEDIUM.** Place lobster tails on grill, shell-side down, 3 or 4 inches above fire. Cook about 15 minutes. Brush generously with melted butter or margarine. Turn and cook 3 minutes longer. Shell is bright red when lobster is done. Season with coarse, freshly ground black pepper and salt to taste. Serve with melted butter or margarine and lemon wedges. Leftovers can be frozen.

Char-grilled Rock Lobster Tails

49

Rainbow trout is an epicure's dream when cooked over a hot fire. There is nothing so fleeting as the delectable flavor of fresh fish. The sooner this flavor can be captured the better.

For campers-out, for one-day fishing trips, for summer colonists at the seashore or near a fresh water stream where small fish abound, Big Boy Portable Barbecue Equipment brings fish from water to table at the height of superb flavor. If you have never tasted brook trout, snappers, small mackerel, bluefish or flounder that have been barbecued, then you have never tasted fish at all! The hot fire coaxes out an enchanting aroma and turns the lustrous surfaces of the raw fish to a sizzling golden brown!

Gourmets insist that heads be left on. Tender-hearted diners prefer not to look the fish in the eye. The choice is yours. Allow one or two whole fish per person.

grilled small whole fish

Select small, whole fish. Have fish cleaned and if desired, have head removed. Wash fish thoroughly and pat dry with paper towels. Rub fish with oil, butter or margarine or make a thin paste of equal parts of flour and cooking oil. Season to taste with salt and pepper. Coat each fish with the mixture. Place fish on grill or in hinged broiler as shown in photo at right. Barbecue over **MEDIUM** heat for 3 to 4 minutes; turn fish once and continue to barbecue for another 3 or 4 minutes.

fish in the spit basket

Prepare fish as for Grilled Small Whole Fish.

FOR CHARCOAL BARBECUING: Heap briquets slightly at rear of fire box. Place an aluminum foil drip pan (see page 14) in front of briquets.*

FOR GAS BARBECUING: Remove grill, turn gas to **HIGH** and light the flame. Turn heat to **MEDIUM.** *

*Rub the spit basket with cooking oil to prevent fish from sticking and put the spit basket on the spit rod. Arrange the fish in a single layer in the basket, alternating head and tail ends for better use of space. Adjust the cover of the basket, being sure that it is not too tight, or it will tear the skin. Attach the spit and start the motor. Barbecue 10 to 15 minutes, depending on thickness of fish. Brush occasionally with butter to keep fish moist. Fish is done when it flakes easily with a fork. Baste, during the last 5 minutes, with melted butter or margarine. Before serving, sprinkle with salt and pepper.

Grilled Small Whole Fish $\longrightarrow$

A leviathan of a striped bass occupies the entire length of the spit as it rotates over the fire to the flavor peak of doneness.

barbecued large whole fish

When you catch the one that usually gets away and triumphantly bring your record-breaker over the side of the boat, what a joy it is to remember that the Big Boy unit is ready to barbecue the fish on the revolving spit over a hot fire, to tender, flaky perfection! For a real treat, try it smoked.

Striped bass, tuna, bluefish, salmon, large mackerel, mullet, pike and weakfish are some of the fish you can barbecue, whole, on a spit. Clean a fish weighing 3 lbs. or more and remove the head. Allow about ½ pound per person. Using small, nail-size skewers and twine, lace up the cavity tightly, see photo. If the fish is a whopper, it may be advisable to tie it around the body with twine spaced at half-inch intervals for the entire length of the fish to prevent it from falling from the spit or breaking apart.

Place the fish on the spit and test for balance (see page 17). Be sure the tines of the spit forks are firmly inserted in the fish.

FOR CHARCOAL BARBECUING: Heap briquets slightly at the rear of the fire box. Place an aluminum foil drip pan (see page 14) in front of the briquets.*

FOR GAS BARBECUING: Remove grill, turn gas to **HIGH** and light the flame. Turn heat to **MEDIUM.***

*Attach the spit and start the motor. During barbecuing brush the fish frequently with melted butter or margarine to keep the surface moist. The butter may be herb-flavored, if you like, with marjoram, oregano or rosemary. Barbecue 15 to 20 minutes, depending on the size of the fish. Fish is done when it flakes easily with a fork. Remove from spit and sprinkle with salt and pepper. Large fish can be stuffed with bread stuffing or your favorite stuffing if desired.

Barbecue liver and bacon? It's really unusual, but why not? The delicate flavor of liver is enhanced by barbecuing.

liver, bacon and onions

Use calf or very young beef liver and have it cut ½ inch thick. Liver should be at room temperature when barbecuing begins. Wash the liver and dry on paper towels. Have bacon thickly sliced so it will not shrink too much during cooking. Select large Spanish or Bermuda onions. Peel and slice them about ½ inch thick. Brush slices with melted butter or margarine. Use firm tomatoes and quarter but do not peel them.

FOR CHARCOAL BARBECUING: When briquets are coated with gray ash and very hot, space them ½ to ¾ inch apart over the gravel to avoid flame-up (see page 11).*

FOR GAS BARBECUING: Remove grill, turn gas to **HIGH** and light the flame. Preheat Bar-B-Rocks on **HIGH** for about 3 minutes. Then turn heat to **MEDIUM**.*

*Rub the grill with cooking oil. Arrange liver and onion slices on the grill.

Barbecue for about 5 minutes. Turn the liver and onion slices and add the tomatoes and bacon. Barbecue about 5 minutes longer. During the last few minutes put onions and bacon on top of liver to blend flavors. To test that liver is cooked just right, make a slit in the meat with a sharp knife. It should be slightly pink inside. Avoid overcooking or it will dry out.

barbecued corn

Select tender sweet corn in the husks. Strip husks down to end of cob. Do not tear off. Remove silk. If desired, let stand in salted ice water 20 minutes to 1 hour; then drain well. Brush corn with softened butter or margarine and sprinkle with salt and coarse, freshly ground black pepper. Bring husks up around corn. Be sure entire ear is covered. Kernels are exposed in pictures to illustrate the following barbecue methods:

METHOD 1. Prepare corn as above. Secure husks in 3 places with thin florist's wire.

FOR CHARCOAL BARBECUING: Lay corn on top of hot briquets.*

FOR GAS BARBECUING: Preheat Bar-B-Rocks on **HIGH** for about 3 minutes and turn heat to **MEDIUM**. Place grill in position and place corn on grill.*

*Barbecue 10 to 12 minutes; turn a quarter turn 4 times during barbecuing. When corn is done, remove wire and husks. Serve at once.

METHOD 2. Prepare corn as above. Wrap each ear securely in a double thickness of heavy duty aluminum foil; twist ends well. Place corn on unit as in Method 1 above. Barbecue about 10 minutes, turning once.

METHOD 3. Prepare corn as above. Slip spit rod through spit basket. Arrange the corn in spit basket. Put basket cover in place. Attach the spit and start the motor. Barbecue about 20 minutes.

barbecued potatoes

Piping hot, fluffy Barbecued Potatoes, topped with plenty of butter and served with char-flavored Barbecued Steak is a combination fit for a king.

Select medium-size baking potatoes; scrub well and pat dry with paper toweling. Rub the skins with soft butter or margarine. Wrap each potato tightly in a double thickness of heavy duty aluminum foil. On a charcoal unit place potatoes directly on top of briquets. On a gas unit place potatoes on the grill over a **MEDIUM**

heat. Barbecue medium-size potatoes 45 to 60 minutes; large potatoes 1 to 1¼ hours. Turn several times during barbecuing. Potatoes are done if they feel soft when gently pressed with an asbestos-gloved thumb. When soft, slit the foil, cut potato in both directions and press gently to break open. Fluff potato with a fork and season to taste with butter or margarine, salt and coarse, freshly ground black pepper. Or, top with a spoonful of sour cream, mixed with finely chopped chives or grated onion.

grilled mushrooms

For each person, place about 6 medium-size mushrooms in a square of double heavy duty aluminum foil. Add about 1½ tablespoons butter or margarine, few grains of salt and coarse, freshly ground black pepper. Wrap foil around mushrooms. Barbecue on **MEDIUM** grill about 4 minutes; turn and cook 4 minutes longer.

stuffed green peppers

Cut a slice from the stem end of 8 green peppers; remove white ribs and seeds. Place each on a double thickness of heavy duty aluminum foil. Fill with canned chili beans. Top each with 1 tablespoon ketchup. Wrap securely in foil. Barbecue on charcoal briquets about 15 minutes or on **MEDIUM** grill about 30 minutes. Turn once during barbecuing.

vegetable medley

For each individual serving, make a 9 inch square of a double thickness of heavy duty aluminum foil. On each square put a slice of peeled, fresh tomato, some cubed, peeled, eggplant, a thin slice of Bermuda or Spanish onion, a sliced mushroom, a few frozen peas and pat of butter or margarine. Sprinkle with salt and fresh, coarsely ground black pepper. Wrap tightly in the foil and barbecue on the charcoal briquets about 15 minutes, or on **MEDIUM** grill 30 to 35 minutes. Turn once during cooking.

barbecued zucchini creole

Slice zucchini squash, crosswise, in ¼ inch slices. Place individual portions on double thicknesses of heavy duty aluminum foil. Add cubed fresh tomato, sliced celery, salt, coarse, freshly ground black pepper, a dash of sugar and a pat of butter or margarine. Wrap foil securely around food. Barbecue on briquets 14 to 16 minutes or on **MEDIUM** grill about 20 to 24 minutes, turning once.

french fried potatoes

Use a 9-inch metal pie pan. (Or, for individual servings, use small aluminum foil pie pans.) Put frozen French fried potatoes in the pan and sprinkle with salt. Place pan on **MEDIUM** grill or directly on the charcoal briquets and barbecue 10 to 15 minutes or until hot and brown. Stir once while heating.

Barbecued Party Apples

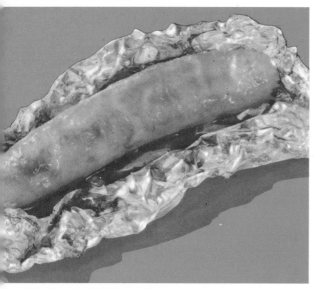

Barbecued Spiced Bananas

barbecued party apples

Core large baking apples. Pare a third of the way down from stem end. Place each on a double thickness of heavy duty aluminum foil. Fill centers with a mixture of sugar and cinnamon. Brush peeled surfaces with pink-tinted light corn syrup and put about ½ tablespoon butter or margarine on each. Wrap very securely in foil. Barbecue 1 hour on **MEDIUM** grill or 25 to 30 minutes on charcoal briquets. Apples are done if they feel soft when gently pressed with an asbestos-gloved thumb.

honey grilled pineapple

Cut a medium-size fresh pineapple into 8 lengthwise wedges. Place each wedge on a double thickness of heavy duty aluminum foil. Pour 1 tablespoon honey over each. Allow to stand ½ hour. Wrap securely in the foil. Barbecue on **MEDIUM** grill 18 to 22 minutes or on charcoal briquets 14 to 16 minutes.

hawaiian oranges

For each serving, peel a seedless orange and separate into sections. Put each sectioned orange on a double thickness of heavy duty aluminum foil. Sprinkle generously with brown sugar. Add a dash of cinnamon, a tablespoon of light rum and a teaspoon of butter or margarine. Wrap securely in foil. Barbecue on **MEDIUM** grill 12 to 15 minutes or on charcoal briquets 8 to 12 minutes.

barbecued spiced bananas

Peel bananas. Place each on a double thickness of heavy duty aluminum foil. Brush with lemon juice. Sprinkle generously with brown sugar; dust with cinnamon or nutmeg; dot with butter or margarine. Wrap the foil securely around the bananas, twisting ends. Barbecue on **MEDIUM** grill 7 to 9 minutes or on charcoal briquets 4 to 5 minutes.

cheese topped french bread

Cut a loaf of French bread in half, lengthwise. Brush generously with melted butter or Garlic Butter (recipe below). Sprinkle liberally with grated Parmesan or sharp Cheddar cheese. Put halves together; wrap securely in a double thickness of heavy duty aluminum foil. Place in the warming oven 15 to 20 minutes, on grill 10 to 12 minutes, or, on charcoal briquets, 6 to 9 minutes. To serve, slice crosswise, to make sandwiches.

GARLIC BUTTER: Place ¼ pound butter or margarine and 1 clove crushed garlic in small saucepan at the edge of the grill where heat is low. When butter is melted, stir and cook 2 minutes. Do not let butter brown.

Cheese Topped French Bread

fan tan garlic rolls

Use ready-to-serve or brown-and-serve packaged Fan Tan Rolls. Remove rolls from the package and place on a double thickness of heavy duty aluminum foil. Brush liberally between cut sections and on top with Garlic Butter (recipe this page). Wrap securely in foil. Place ready-to-serve rolls in the warming oven 15 to 20 minutes, on grill 10 to 12 minutes, or on charcoal briquets 6 to 9 minutes. Place brown-and-serve rolls on the grill 20 to 25 minutes or on charcoal briquets 10 to 12 minutes.

poppy seed bread

Use a small loaf of unsliced white bread. Cut in half lengthwise, almost through to bottom, then crosswise, in eighths. Place on a double thickness of heavy duty aluminum foil. Brush all cut and outside surface with melted butter or Garlic Butter (recipe this page). Sprinkle top sides and cut surfaces liberally with poppy seeds. Wrap securely in foil. Place in warming oven 15 to 20 minutes, on the grill 10 to 12 minutes or on charcoal briquets 6 to 9 minutes. To serve, pull sections apart.

Fan Tan Garlic Rolls

Poppy Seed Bread

fruit spear platter

A beautifully arranged platter of fresh fruit spears is simple to prepare and adds interesting color and texture to a meal. Try serving a platter of fruit in place of vegetables. The fruit is eaten as a finger food. (See photo below)

On a bed of crisp salad green arrange finger-size pieces of chilled watermelon, pineapple, cantaloupe or honeydew melon and bananas, thin unpeeled slices of red apples and quartered, cored, unpeeled pears; place a small whole pineapple in the center of the platter, if desired. Provide small bowls of French dressing, sour cream and cream mayonnaise for "dunking," if desired.

salad dressing for mixed greens

½ *pound Roquefort or blue cheese*
¼ *cup lemon juice*
⅓ *tube anchovy paste*
¼ *cup tarragon vinegar*
2 *tablespoons bottled thick steak sauce*
2 *tablespoons Worcestershire sauce*
3 *tablespoons red table wine*
2 *teaspoons dry mustard*
2 *teaspoons prepared mustard*
Salt to taste
Freshly ground black pepper
⅔ *cup olive oil*
⅔ *cup salad oil*
2 *garlic cloves, if desired*

Put half the cheese in the large bowl of an electric mixer; beat until creamy. Blend in next 8 ingredients and salt and pepper to taste. Gradually add oils. Crumble an equal amount of remaining cheese into each of 2 pint jars with tight-fitting covers. Fill jars with dressing. Store in refrigerator. About an hour before serving, add a garlic clove to each jar and let stand at room temperature. To serve, shake thoroughly; remove garlic, pour over greens and toss. If desired, sprinkle with grated Parmesan cheese and add more salt and pepper. Makes about 2 pints.

golden potato salad

4 cups diced, cold boiled potatoes
1 small onion, chopped
2 tablespoons chopped parsley
1 cup chopped celery
1 teaspoon salt
2 tablespoons light cream
4 tablespoons yellow prepared mustard
2 tablespoons sugar
2 tablespoons vinegar
¼ teaspoon salt
Dash pepper
Crisp salad greens

In a large bowl, put potatoes, onion, parsley, celery and the 1 teaspoon salt and toss lightly. Combine cream and next 5 ingredients and beat with a rotary beater until light and fluffy. Pour over the potato mixture and stir gently until well mixed. Let stand about 1 hour. Line a salad bowl with salad greens and arrange potato salad on top. Makes 6 to 8 servings.

caesar salad

Juice of 2 lemons
½ cup olive oil
¼ cup wine vinegar
1 tablespoon Worcestershire sauce
2 whole garlic cloves, peeled
2 cups ½-inch bread cubes
2 garlic cloves, peeled and crushed
½ cup butter
4 heads crisp romaine*
2 eggs, raw or coddled 2 minutes
¼ cup grated Parmesan cheese
1 small can anchovy fillets, whole or diced
Salt
Coarse, freshly ground black pepper

*Or 3 quarts shredded lettuce or mixed salad greens.

Combine first 5 ingredients; let stand several hours. Remove garlic.

Toast bread cubes on a baking sheet in a moderate oven, 350°F., stirring occasionally, until cubes are lightly browned on all sides. Melt butter with crushed garlic in a large frying pan, stir in toasted bread cubes; continue stirring until cubes absorb butter. Keep warm. Break romaine into a large salad bowl. Break eggs over the romaine; add olive oil mixture. Toss well until all traces of egg disappear. Add cheese, anchovy fillets, toasted cubes and salt to taste. Pepper generously with coarse, freshly ground black pepper. Toss again to mix. Makes 12 servings.

chocolate cake

2 cup sifted cake flour
2 teaspoons baking powder
½ teaspoon baking soda
½ teaspoon salt
½ cup shortening
2 cups firmly packed brown sugar
2 eggs
1 teaspoon vanilla
4 squares unsweetened chocolate, melted
1 cup plus 2 tablespoons milk
Coffee Frosting

Set oven for moderate, 350°F. Grease and flour two 8-inch round cake pans. Sift together flour, baking powder, baking soda and salt. Beat shortening; add sugar gradually; beat until fluffy. Add eggs, one at a time; beat well after each addition; stir in vanilla and chocolate. Add dry ingredients alternately with milk; stir only enough to blend well. Turn into pans. Bake 30 minutes or until cake springs back when lightly pressed with fingertip. Cool in pans 10 to 15 minutes. Remove; cool on a rack. Frost with Coffee Frosting.

COFFEE FROSTING: Combine 2 egg whites, 1½ cups sugar, ½ teaspoon cream of tartar, ⅓ cup strong coffee and 2 teaspoons light corn syrup in top of a double boiler, stir to blend well. Place over boiling water and beat with a rotary beater until frosting holds its shape. Remove from heat; continue beating until frosting stands in peaks.

banana walnut chiffon cake

2¼ cups sifted cake flour
1½ cups sugar
3 teaspoons baking powder
1 teaspoon salt
½ cup cooking oil
5 egg yolks, unbeaten
1 cup mashed ripe bananas
1 tablespoon lemon juice
½ teaspoon cream of tartar
1 cup egg whites
Whipped cream
Chopped walnuts

Set oven for moderately low, 325°F. Sift together flour, sugar, baking powder, and salt. Make a "well" in dry ingredients and add next 4 ingredients in the order listed. Beat until smooth. Add cream of tartar to egg white and whip in a large mixing bowl until they form very stiff peaks. Gradually and gently fold flour mixture into egg whites, just until blended. Do not stir. Turn into an ungreased, 10-inch tube pan. Bake 1 hour and 5 minutes, or until top springs back when lightly touched with the fingertip. Invert pan; let cake hang until cold.

To remove, loosen from sides and tube of pan with spatula. Frost with whipped cream and garnish with nuts.

old-fashioned strawberry shortcake

2 cups sifted flour
3 teaspoons baking powder
½ teaspoon salt
2 tablespoons sugar
½ cup shortening
1 egg, well beaten
⅓ cup milk (about)
2 quarts strawberries
Sugar
2 tablespoons butter or margarine
Sweetened whipped cream

Set oven for very hot, 450°F. Grease an 8-inch round cake pan.

Mix and sift flour, baking powder, salt and the 2 tablespoons sugar. Cut in shortening with a pastry blender or 2 knives until mixture looks like coarse cornmeal. Combine egg and milk; stir into flour mixture to make a soft dough. If dough is too stiff, add a little more milk. Pat or roll out into an 8-inch circle; place in pan. Bake 15 to 18 minutes, until brown.

Meanwhile, wash and hull berries; slice and sprinkle with sugar to taste.

When cake is done, remove from pan; split and spread with butter. Put lower half on a serving plate and cover with half the berries. Top with remaining cake and berries. Serve with whipped cream. Makes 6 to 8 servings.

NOTE: You may use two 10-ounce packages sliced frozen strawberries in place of the fresh strawberries.

apple pie

Pastry for a 2-crust pie or 1 package pie
   crust mix
5 or 6 tart apples, pared and sliced
1 cup sugar
2 teaspoons flour
Dash nutmeg
½ teaspoon cinnamon
2 tablespoons butter or margarine

Set the oven for hot, 400°F. Prepare pastry. Roll out half of it in a circle about 12 inches in diameter and ⅛ inch thick. Line a 9-inch pie pan with the pastry and trim ¼ inch from rim. Arrange apples in pan. Mix sugar, flour and spices; sprinkle over apples. Dot with butter. Roll out remaining pastry about 11 inches in diameter and ⅛ inch thick. Cut slit for steam to escape. Adjust pastry over apples and trim ½ inch from rim of pan. Fold edge of top pastry under edge of lower pastry. Press edges together and flute or crimp. Bake 45 minutes or until crust browns and apples are tender.

Decorate the pie with "apples" cut from slices of processed cheese and sprinkled with paprika.

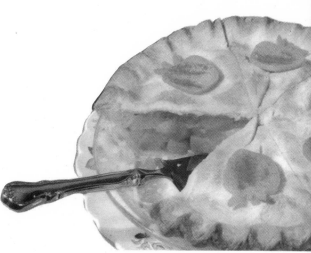

fruit drink coolers

Serve cool fruit drinks to guests as they watch the chef perform at the grill and serve them with the meal. These drinks belong in the easy-does-it department.

Fruit drinks go over big with your guests and it's easy to have a variety when you take advantage of the frozen and canned juices which are available. Keep frozen concentrates in the freezer until serving time and chill canned juices thoroughly. At serving time, prepare the juices as directed on the cans and pour into glasses over ice cubes. To keep drinks from becoming watery, freeze juice in ice cube trays and use the juice cubes for cooling the drinks.

Fruit kababs (shown in photo) make nice appetizers to serve with the drinks. Thread small fresh and canned fruits such as grapes, preserved kumquats, and sweet or maraschino cherries on bamboo skewers. Push the fruits to the center of the skewer leaving the ends free. Insert one end of the skewer into a bowl of crushed ice.

Fruit Drink Coolers

round-up coffee

An old-fashioned coffee pot on the grill is a welcome sight to everyone who believes that a barbecue is not complete unless there is a never-ending supply of piping hot coffee. Brewing coffee in a pot differs from procedures used for other coffee makers but the art is easy to master.

For good clear coffee you need coarsely ground coffee and a square of 4 thicknesses of cheesecloth. The cloth should be 18 to 36 inches square depending on the quantity of coffee you make. Measurements, below, are given for large cups which hold about 7 ounces and you'd better count on 1½ cups per person.

For 10 cups, use 1½ cups ground coffee and 2¼ quarts of cold water.

For 15 cups, use 2¼ cups ground coffee and 3¾ quarts of cold water.

For 25 cups, use 3¾ cups ground coffee and 6¼ quarts of cold water.

Dampen the cheesecloth in cold water and spread it out; put coffee in the center. Gather up edges to form a bag and tie with twine, allowing enough room for the coffee to expand. Put the bag and water in the pot. Place over low heat and stir every 3 to 5 minutes. As soon as coffee comes to a boiling point, remove from heat. Lift out bag. Keep coffee hot until serving time.

index

general

barbecue sauces

beverages

breads

desserts and fruits

fire, how to build

fish and seafood

fire, how to build

meats

use a drip pan for these recipes: